According to Promise

According to Promise

or

The Lord's Method of Dealing with His Chosen People

by

Charles H. Spurgeon

The Gospel Hour, Inc., Oliver B. Greene, Director
P.O. Box 2024, Greenville, South Carolina

Printed in the United States of America

Contents

A Sieve Needed

IT is very important to be able to distinguish between things that differ, for appearances are not to be relied upon. Things which seem to be alike may yet be the opposite of each other. A scorpion may be like an egg, and a stone like a piece of bread; but they are far from being the same. Like may be very unlike. Especially is this the case in spiritual things, and therefore it behoves us to be on our guard.

It would be very difficult to say how far a man may go in religion, and yet die in his sins; how much he may look like an heir of heaven, and yet be a child of wrath. Many unconverted men have a belief which is similar to faith, and yet it is not true faith. Certain persons exhibit pious affections which have the warmth of spiritual love, but are quite destitute of gracious life. Every grace can be counterfeited, even as jewels can be imitated. As paste gems are wonderfully like the real stones, so sham graces are marvellously like the work of the Spirit of God. In soul matters a man will need to have all his wits about him, or he will soon deceive his own heart. It is to be feared that many are already mistaken, and will never discover their delusion till they lift up their eyes in the world of woe, where their disappointment will be terrible indeed.

The dead child of nature may be carefully washed by its mother, but this will not make it the living child of grace. The life of God within the soul creates an infinite difference between the man who has it and the man who has it not; and the point is, to make sure that we have this life.

Are YOU sure that you have it ?

It will be an awful thing to cry, " Peace, peace," where there is no peace, and to prophesy smooth things for yourself, and make your heart easy, and lull your conscience to slumber, and never to wake out of the sleep till a clap of the thunder of judgment shall startle you out of presumption into endless horror.

I desire to help my reader in the business of self-examination. I would have him go further than examination, and attain to such abundance of grace, that his holy and happy state shall become a witness to himself.

The first part of this little book is meant to be a sieve to separate the chaff from the wheat. Let my friend use it upon himself; it may be the best day's work he has ever done. He who looked into his accounts and found that his business was a losing one was saved from bankruptcy. This may happen also to my reader. Should he, however, discover that his heavenly trade is prospering, it will be a great comfort to him. No man can lose by honestly searching his own heart.

FRIEND, TRY IT AT ONCE.

The Two Seeds

"It is written, that Abraham had two sons, the one by a bondmaid, the other by a freewoman. But he who was of the bondwoman was born after the flesh; but he of the freewoman was by promise."— Galatians iv. 22, 23.

ABRAHAM had two sons. Ishmael and Isaac were beyond all dispute veritable sons of Abraham. Yet, one of them inherited the covenant blessing, and the other was simply a prosperous man of the world. *See how close these two were together!* They were born in the same society, called the same great patriarch "father," and sojourned in the same encampment with him. Yet, Ishmael was a stranger to the covenant, while Isaac was the heir of the promise. How little is there in blood and birth!

A more remarkable instance than this happened a little afterwards; for Esau and Jacob were born of the same mother, at the same birth, yet is it written, "Jacob have I loved, and Esau have I hated." One became gracious, and the other profane. So closely may two come together, and yet so widely may they be separated! Verily, it is not only that two shall be in one bed, and the one shall be taken, and the other left; but, two shall come into the world at the same moment, and yet one of them will take up his inheritance with God, and the other will for a morsel of meat sell his birthright. We may be in the same church, baptized in the same water,

seated at the same communion table, singing the
same psalm, and offering the same prayer ; and yet
we may be of two races as opposed as the seed of
the woman and the seed of the serpent.

Abraham's two sons are declared by Paul to be
the types of two races of men, who are much alike,
and yet widely differ. *They are unlike in their origin.*
They were both sons of Abraham ; but Ishmael,
the child of Hagar, was the offspring of Abraham
upon ordinary conditions : he was born after the
flesh. Isaac, the son of Sarah, was not born by
the strength of nature ; for his father was more than
a hundred years old, and his mother was long past
age. He was given to his parents by the Lord, and
was born *according to the promise* through faith.
This is a grave distinction, and it marks off the true
child of God from him who is only so by profession. *The promise* lies at the bottom of the
distinction, and the power which goes to accomplish
the promise creates and maintains the difference.
Hence *the promise*, which is our inheritance, is also
our test and touchstone.

Let us use the test at once by seeing whether we
have been wrought upon by the power which fulfils
the promise. Let me ask a few questions,—How
were you converted ? Was it by yourself, by the
persuasion of men, by carnal excitement ; or was it
by the operation of the Spirit of God ? You profess
to have been born again. Whence came that new
birth ? Did it come from God in consequence of his
eternal purpose and promise, or did it come out of
yourself ? Was it your old nature trying to do better,

and working itself up to its best form? If so, you are Ishmael. Or was it that you, being spiritually dead, and having no strength whatever to rise out of your lost estate, were visited by the Spirit of God, who put forth his divine energy, and caused life from heaven to enter into you? Then you are Isaac. All will depend upon the commencement of your spiritual life, and the source from which that life at first proceeded. If you began in the flesh, you have gone on in the flesh, and in the flesh you will die.

Have you never read, "That which is born of the flesh is flesh"? Before long the flesh will perish, and from it you will reap corruption. Only "that which is born of the Spirit is spirit"; the joy is that the spirit will live, and of it you will reap life everlasting. Whether you are a professor of religion or not, I beseech you, ask yourself—*Have I* felt the power of *the Spirit of God?*

Is the life that is within you the result of the fermentation of your own natural desires? Or is it a new element, infused, imparted, implanted from above? Is your spiritual life a heavenly creation? Have you been created anew in Christ Jesus? Have you been born again by divine power?

Ordinary religion is nature gilded over with a thin layer of what is thought to be grace. Sinners have polished themselves up, and brushed off the worst of the rust and the filth, and they think their old nature is as good as new. This touching-up and repairing of the old man is all very well; but it falls short of what is needed. You may wash the face and hands of Ishmael as much as you please, but you cannot make him into Isaac. You may improve nature, and the more you do so the better for certain temporary purposes; but you cannot raise it into grace. There is a distinction at the very fountain-head between the stream which rises in the bog of fallen humanity, and the river which proceeds from the throne of God.

Do not forget that our Lord himself said, " *Ye must be born again.*" If you have not been born again from above, all your church-going, or your chapel-going, stands for nothing. Your prayers and your tears, your Bible-readings and all that have come from yourself only, can only lead to yourself. Water will naturally rise as high as its source, but no higher: that which begins with human nature will rise to human nature; but to the divine nature it cannot reach. Was your new birth natural or supernatural? Was it of the will of man or of God? Much will depend upon your answer to that question.

Between the child of God and the mere professor there is a distinction as to origin of the most serious sort. Isaac was born *according to promise.* Ishmael was not of promise, but of the course of nature. Where nature's strength suffices there is no promise; but when human energy fails, the word of the Lord comes in. God had said that Abraham should have a son of Sarah; Abraham believed it, and rejoiced therein, and Isaac was born as the result of the divine promise, by the power of God. There could have been no Isaac if there had been no promise, and there can be no true believer apart from the promise of grace, and the grace of the promise.

Gentle reader, here let me enquire as to your salvation. Are you saved by what you have done? Is your religion the product of your own natural strength? Do you feel equal to all that salvation may require? Do you conclude yourself to be in a safe and happy condition because of your natural excellence and moral ability? Then you are after the manner of Ishmael, and to you the inheritance will not come; for it is not an inheritance according to the flesh, but according to promise.

If, on the other hand, you say,—"*My hope lies only in the promise of God. He has set forth that promise in the person of his Son Jesus to every sinner that believeth in him; and I do believe in him, therefore I trust and believe that the Lord will fulfil his promise and bless me. I look for heavenly blessedness, not as the result of my own efforts, but as the gift of God's free favour. My hope is fixed alone upon the free and gratuitous love of God to guilty men, by the which he has given his Son Jesus Christ to put away sin, and to bring in everlasting righteousness for those who deserve it not,*"—then this is another sort of language from that of the Ishmaelites, who say "We have Abraham to our father." You have now learned to speak as Isaac speaks. The difference may seem small to the careless, but it is great indeed. Hagar, the slave-mother, is a very different person from Sarah, the princess. To the one there is no covenant promise, to the other the blessing belongs for evermore. Salvation by works is one thing; salvation by grace is another. Salvation by human strength is far removed from salvation by divine power : and salvation by our own resolve is the opposite of salvation by the promise of God.

Put yourself under this enquiry, and see to which family you belong. Are you of Ishmael or of Isaac?

If you find that you are like Isaac, born according to the promise, remember that your name is "Laughter"; for that is the interpretation of the Hebrew name Isaac. Take care that you rejoice with joy unspeakable and full of glory. Your new birth is a wonderful thing. If both Abraham and Sarah laughed at the thought of Isaac, you may certainly do so concerning yourself. There are times when, if I sit alone and think of the grace of God to me, the most undeserving of all his creatures, I am ready to laugh and cry at the same time for joy that ever the Lord should have looked in love and favour upon me. Yes, and every child of God must have felt the working of that Isaac nature within his soul, filling his mouth with laughter, because the Lord hath done great things for him.

Mark well the difference between the two seeds, from their very beginning.

Ishmael comes of man, and by man. Isaac comes *by God's promise*. Ishmael is the child of Abraham's flesh. Isaac is Abraham's child, too; but then the power of God comes in, and from the weakness of his parents it is made clear that he is of the Lord,—a gift according to promise. True faith is assuredly the act of the man who believes ;

true repentance is the act of the man who repents;
yet both faith and repentance may with unquestion-
able correctness be described as the work of God,
even as Isaac is the son of Abraham and Sarah,
and yet he is still more the gift of God. The Lord
our God, who bids us believe, also enables us to
believe. All that we do acceptably the Lord worketh
in us; yea, the very will to do it is of his working.
No religion is worth a farthing which is not essentially the outflow of the man's own heart; and yet
it must beyond question be the work of the Holy
Ghost who dwells within him.

O friend, if what you have within you is natural,
and only natural, it will not save you! The inward
work must be supernatural; it must come of God,
or it will miss the covenant blessing. A gracious
life will be your own, even as Isaac was truly the
child of Abraham; but still more it will be of God;
for "Salvation is of the Lord." We must be born
from above. Concerning all our religious feelings
and actions, we must be able to say, "Lord, thou
hast wrought all our works in us."

The Two Lives

" Neither, because they are the seed of Abraham, are they all children: but, In Isaac shall thy seed be called. That is, They which are the children of the flesh, these are not the children of God : but the children of the promise are counted for the seed. For this is the word of promise, At this time will I come, and Sarah shall have a son."—Romans ix. 7, 8, 9.

ISHMAEL and Isaac differed as to origin, and hence there was a difference *in their nature* which showed itself in their lives, and was chiefly seen in their relation to *the promise.*

According to the birth so will be the life which comes of it. In the case of the man who is only what he made himself to be, there will be only what nature gives him ; but in the case of the man who is created anew by the Spirit of God, there will be signs following. " Of him are ye in Christ Jesus, who of God is made unto us wisdom, and righteousness, and sanctification, and redemption : as it is written, He that glorieth, let him glory in the Lord." There will be in the new-born man that which the new life brings with it : in the natural man there will be nothing of the kind.

Ishmael exhibited certain of the natural character-istics of Abraham joined with those of his slave mother. He was a princely man like his father, and inherited the patriarch's noble bearing; but Isaac had the faith of his father, and was in the succession as to holy inward spiritual life. As the heir of the promise, Isaac remains with his father Abraham, while Ishmael is forming camps of his own in the wilderness. Isaac seeks alliance with the olden stock in Mesopotamia ; but Ishmael's mother takes him a wife out of Egypt, which was very natural, since she came from Egypt herself. Like will to like. Isaac meditated in the field at eventide, for his conversation was with sacred things ; but Ishmael contended with all comers, for he minded earthly things. Meditation is not for the wild man, whose hand is against every man, and every man's hand against him. Isaac surrendered himself as a sacrifice to God ; but you see nothing of that kind in Ishmael. Self-sacrifice is not for Ishmael ; he is rather a killer and a slayer than a lamb that presents itself to God. So you shall find, that if you are religiously trained and tutored, and become "pious," as they call it, and yet are not renewed in heart, nor visited by the Holy Ghost, you will not live the secret life of the child of God. You may show many of the outward marks of a Christian ; you may be able to sing, and to pray, and to quote Scripture, and perhaps to tell some little bits of imaginary experience ; but you must be born again to know in very deed and truth the fellowship of the saints, communion in secret with the living God, and the yielding of yourself to him as your reason-able service. The child of the promise abides with God's people, and counts it his privilege to be numbered with them. The child of the promise feels that he is in the best company when no man can see or be seen, but when the Great Invisible draws near to him and holds converse with him. The child of the promise, and he only, is able to go up to the top of Moriah, there to be bound upon the altar, and to yield himself up to God. I mean by this last, that only he who is born of the Spirit will yield himself wholly to God, and love the Lord better than life itself. Your nature and conduct will be according to your origin; and therefore I pray that you may begin aright, so that as you profess to be a child of the kingdom, you may prove to be a true-born heir.

Ishmael, who was born after the flesh, the child of the bondwoman, must always bear the servile taint. The child of a slave is not free-born. Ishmael is not, cannot be, what Isaac is—the child of the free woman. Now mark: I do not say that Ishmael ever desired to be like Isaac; I do not say that he felt himself to be a loser by differing from Isaac; but, indeed, he was so. The man who is labouring for self-salvation by his own doings, feelings, and self-denials, may be proudly ignorant of his servile state; he may even boast that he was born free, and was never in bondage to any; and yet he spends his whole life in servitude. He never knows what liberty means, what content means, what delight in God means. He wonders when men talk about "full assurance of faith." He judges that they must be presumptuous. *He* has scarcely time to breathe between the cracks of the whip. He has done so much, but he must do so much more; he has suffered so much, but he must suffer so much more. He has never come into "the rest which remaineth for the people of God;" for he is born of the bond-woman, and his spirit is ever in bondage. On the other hand, he that is born of the free woman, and understands that salvation is of the grace of God from first to last, and that where God has given his grace he does not take it back, for "the gifts and calling of God are without repentance"—such a man accepting the finished work of Christ, and knowing his acceptance in the Beloved, rests in the Lord, and rejoices exceedingly. His life and his spirit are filled with joy and peace, for he was born free, and he is free, yea, free indeed.

Does my reader understand the freedom of the child of God? or is he still in servitude under the law, afraid of punishment, afraid of being sent away into the wilderness? If you are in this latter case, you have not received *the promise*, or you would know that such a thing could not be. To Isaac, the child of *the promise*, the heritage belongs, and he abides for ever, without fear of being cast out.

Those that are born as Ishmael was, according to the flesh, and whose religion is a matter of their own power and strength, mind earthly things, as Ishmael did. Only those that are born from above *through the promise* according to faith will, like Isaac, mind heavenly things. See how the naturally religious man minds earthly things. He is very regular at his place of worship; but while he is there he thinks of his business, his house, or his farm. Does he enjoy the worship of God? Not he! There is a sermon. Does he receive with meek-ness the engrafted word which is able to save his soul? Not he! He criticizes it as if it were a political harangue. He gives his money to the cause of God as others do. Of course he does; for he feels that he has to quiet his conscience, and to keep up his good repute: but does he care for the glory of God? By no means. If he did he would give more than money. His heart's prayers would go up for the progress of the kingdom. Does he sigh and cry because of the sins of the times? Do you find him alone with God pouring out his heart in anguish because even in his own family there are those that are not converted to God? Did you ever see in him a high and holy joy when sinners are converted—an exultation because the kingdom of Christ is coming? Oh no, he never rises to that. All the service of God is outward to him: into the core and heart of spiritual things he has never entered, and he never can. The carnal mind, even when it is religious, is still enmity against God, and it is not reconciled to God, neither indeed can it be. There must be a spiritual mind created in the man, he must become a new creature in Christ Jesus, before he can appreciate, understand, and enjoy spiritual things.

To come back to where we started: "Ye must be born again." We must be born of the Spirit: we must receive a supernatural life by being quickened from our death in sin. We cannot bear the fruit of the Spirit till we have the inner life of the Spirit. Ishmael will be Ishmael; and Isaac will be Isaac. As the man is, such will his conduct be. The man of sight, and reason, and human power, may do his best as Ishmael did ; but only the child of the promise will rise to the life and walk of faith as Isaac did.

"*Hard lines*," says one. Sometimes it is a great blessing to have those hard lines drawn, and drawn very straight, too. By this means we may be set on the right track for eternity. One said the other day to a friend of mine, "I once went to hear Mr. Spurgeon, and when I went into the Tabernacle if you had asked me about myself I should have judged that I was as religious a man as ever lived in Newington, and as good a man, certainly, as ever made part of a congregation ; but all this was reversed when I heard the gospel that day. I came out of the place with every feather plucked out of me. I felt myself the most wretched sinner that could be on the face of the earth, and I said I will never go to hear that man again, for he has spoiled me altogether." "Yes," he said, "but that was the best thing that could have happened to me. I was made to look away from myself, and all that I could do, to God and to his omnipotent grace, and to understand that I must pass under my Creator's hand again, or I could never see his face with joy." I hope my reader knows this truth for himself : a solemn truth it is. Even as first of all God made Adam, so must he make us over again, or else we can never bear his image, nor behold his glory. We must come under the influence of *the promise*, and live upon the promise, or our lives will never be guided by right principles, nor directed to right ends.

Differing Hopes

"And as for Ishmael, I have heard thee: Behold, I have blessed him, and will make him fruitful, and will multiply him exceedingly; twelve princes shall he beget, and I will make him a great nation. But my covenant will I establish with Isaac, which Sarah shall bear unto thee at this set time in the next year."—Genesis xvii. 20, 21.

IT is not at all wonderful that two persons, so different in their birth and nature as Ishmael and Isaac were, became very different in *their hopes*. To Isaac the covenant promise became the pole-star of his being; but for Ishmael no such light had arisen. Ishmael aimed at large things, for he was the natural son of one of the greatest of men; but Isaac looked for still higher objects, because he was the child of the promise, and the inheritor of the covenant of grace which the Lord had made with Abraham.

Ishmael, with his high and daring spirit, looked to found a nation which should never be subdued, a race untamable as the wild ass of the desert; and his desire has been abundantly granted: the Bedaween Arabs are to this day true copies of their great ancestor. Ishmael in life and death realized the narrow, earthly hopes for which he looked; but on the roll of those who saw the day of Christ, and died in hope of the glory, his name is not entered. Isaac, on the other hand, saw far ahead, even to the day of Christ. He looked for a city which hath foundations, whose Builder and Maker is God.

Ishmael, like Passion, in "Pilgrim's Progress," had his best things here below ; but Isaac, like Patience, waited for his best things for the future. His treasures were not in the tent and in the field, but in the "things not seen as yet." He had received the great covenant promise, and there he found greater riches than all the flocks of Nebaioth could minister to him. Upon his eye the day-star of promise had shone, and he expected a full noon of blessing in the fulness of the appointed time. The promise so operated upon him as to direct the current of his thoughts and expectations. Is it so with you, my reader? Have *you* received and embraced the promise of eternal life? Are *you*, therefore, hoping for things not seen as yet? Have you an eye to that which none can behold except believers in the faithfulness of God? Have you left the rut of present sensual perception for the way of faith in the unseen and eternal?

No doubt the reception of the promise, and the enjoyment of its hopes, influenced the mind and temper of Isaac, so that he was of a restful spirit. For him there were no wars and fightings. He yielded the present, and waited for the future. Isaac felt that as he was born after the promise it was for God to bless him, and to fulfil the promise that he had made concerning him ; and so he remained with Abraham and kept himself aloof from the outside world. He both quietly hoped and patiently waited for the blessing of God. His eye was on the future, on the great nation yet to come, the promised land, and the yet more glorious promised

seed in whom all the nations of the earth would be
blessed.   For all this he looked to God alone, wisely
judging that he who gave the promise would himself see to its fulfilment.   Because of this faith he
was none the less active ; yet he manifested none
of the proud self-reliance which was so apparent in
Ishmael.   He was energetic in his own way, with a
calm confidence in God, and a quiet submission to
his supreme will.   Year after year he held on in the
separated life, and braved unarmed the danger
which arose from his heathen neighbours—dangers
which Ishmael confronted with his sword and with
his bow.   His trust was in that voice which said,
" Touch not mine anointed, and do my prophets no
harm."   He was a man of peace, and yet he lived
as securely as his warlike brother.   His faith in the
promise gave him hope of security, yea, gave him
security itself, though the Canaanite was still in the
land.

Thus does *the promise* operate upon our present
life by creating in us an elevation of spirit, a life
above visible surroundings, a calm and heavenly
frame of mind.   Isaac finds his bow and his spear
in his God, Jehovah is his shield and his exceeding
great reward.   Without a foot of land to call his
own, dwelling as a sojourner and a stranger in the
land which God had given him by promise, Isaac
was content to live upon the promise and count
himself rich in joys to come.   His remarkably
quiet and equable spirit, while leading the strange
unearthly life of one of the great pilgrim fathers,
sprang out of his simple faith in the promise of the

unchanging God. Hope, kindled by a divine promise, affects the entire life of a man in his inmost thoughts, ways, and feelings : it may seem to be of less importance than correct moral deportment, but in truth it is of vital moment, not only in itself, but in that which it produces upon the mind, heart, and life. The secret hope of a man is a truer test of his condition before God than the acts of any one day, or even the public devotions of a year. Isaac pursues his quiet holy way till he grows old and blind, and gently falls asleep trusting in his God, who had revealed himself to him, and had called him to be his friend, and had said, "Sojourn in this land, and I will be with thee and bless thee, and in thy seed shall all the nations of the earth be blessed."

As a man's hopes are, such is he. If his hope is in the promise of God, it is, it must be, well with him.

Reader, what are *your* hopes? "Why," says one, "I am waiting till a relative dies, and then I shall be rich. I have great expectations." Another hopes in his steadily growing trade ; and a third expects much from a promising speculation. Hopes which can be realized in a dying world are mere mockeries. Hopes which have no outlook beyond the grave are dim windows for a soul to look through. Happy he who believes the promise, and feels assured of its fulfilment to himself in due time, and leaves all else in the hands of infinite wisdom and love. Such hope will endure trials, conquer temptations, and enjoy heaven below.

When Christ died on the cross our hopes began, when he rose they were confirmed, when he went up on high they began to be fulfilled, when he comes a second time they will be realized. In this world we shall have pilgrim's fare, and a table spread in the presence of our enemies ; and in the world to come we shall possess the land which floweth with milk and honey, a land of peace and joy, where the sun shall no more go down, neither shall the moon withdraw herself. Till then we hope, and our hope layeth hold upon *the promise*.

Persecution Consequent on the Promise

" Now we, brethren, as Isaac was, are the children of promise.
But as then he that was born after the flesh persecuted him that was
born after the Spirit, even so it is now."—Gal. iv. 28, 29.

WHEN brothers differ so greatly as Ishmael and Isaac, it is not surprising if they fall out, and indulge unkind feelings. Ishmael was older than Isaac, and when the time came for Isaac to be weaned, his mother, Sarah, saw the son of the bondwoman mocking her child: so early had the difference of birth and condition begun to display itself. This may serve us as an indication of what we may expect if we possess the God-given life, and are heirs according to the promise. Those who are under the bondage of the law cannot love those who are free-born by the gospel, and in some way or other they soon display their enmity.

We are not now thinking of the hostility between the wicked world and the church, but of that which exists between men of a merely natural religion, and those who are born of God. We speak not of the Philistines opposing Isaac, but of his brother Ishmael mocking him. Keenest of all is this opposition of the externally religious, to those who are born from above and worship God in spirit and in truth. Many precious children of God have suffered bitterly from the cruel hatred of those who professed to be their brethren.

Probably the motive of Ishmael was *envy;* he could not endure that the little one should have preeminence over himself. He seemed to say, " This is the heir, and therefore I hate him." Perhaps he mocked Isaac's *heir-ship*, and boasted that he had as good a right to the estate as ever the child of the promise could have. Thus do mere professors envy the condition of believers, and reckon themselves to be quite as good as the best of those who hope to be saved by the grace of God. They do not desire the grace of God themselves, and yet, like the dog in the manger, they cannot bear that others should have it : they envy the saints their hope, their peace of mind, and their enjoyment of the favour of God. If any of you find it so, be not in the least surprised.

The envy of Ishmael displayed itself most at the great feast which had been made at his brother's weaning ; and even thus do formalists, like the elder brother in the parable, become most provoked when there is most occasion for rejoicing in connection with the Father's beloved child. The music and dancing of the true family are gall and wormwood to proud base-born professors. When full assurance is weaned from doubt, and holy delight is weaned from the world, then the carnal religionist puts on a sneer, and calls the godly mad, or fanatical, or murmurs with sullen sarcasm, " Poor fools ! let them alone ; they are a sadly deluded crew." People who are religious but not truly regenerated, who are working and hoping to be saved by their own merits, usually exhibit a bitter hatred towards those who are born of the promise.

Sometimes they mock their *feebleness*. May be Ishmael called Isaac a mere baby, just weaned. So are believers a feeble folk, and exceedingly likely to excite the derision of those who think themselves strong-minded. Isaac could not deny that he was weak, neither can believers deny that they are faulty, and are subject to infirmities which may put them under just censure : but the world makes more of this than justice will allow, and mocks at saints for weaknesses which in others would be overlooked. We must not think it a strange thing if our insignificance and imperfection should set proud and self-righteous Pharisees jeering at us and our Gospel.

Frequently the sport is raised by the believer's *pretensions*. Isaac was called "the heir," and Ishmael could not bear to hear it. "Look," says the legalist, "yonder man was not long ago a known sinner; now he says he has believed in Jesus Christ, and therefore he declares that he knows himself to be saved and accepted, and sure of heaven. Did you ever hear of such presumption?" He who hugs his chains hates the presence of a free man. He who refuses the mercy of God because he proudly trusts his own merits, is angry with the man who rejoices to be saved by grace.

Perhaps the little Isaac, the child of such aged parents, seemed *odd and strange* to the young half-bred Egyptian. No person is so much a foreigner to his fellow-men as a man born from above. To live by faith upon the promise of God ought to seem the most proper and natural thing in the world ; but it is not so esteemed : on the contrary, men count those to be strange beings who believe in God, and act upon such a belief. Wretched boys in the streets still hoot at foreigners, and men of the world still jest at true believers, because of their unworldly spirit and conduct. To us this is a testimony for good, for our Lord said, " If ye were of the world, the world would love his own ; but because ye are not of the world, but I have chosen you out of the world, therefore the world hateth you."

In a thousand ways, many of them so petty as to be unworthy of mention, the believer can be made to bear " trials of cruel mockings," and he ought to be prepared so to do. After all, it is but a small matter to be persecuted nowadays ; for the fires of Smithfield are quenched, the Lollards' tower contains no prisoners, and not even a thumb-screw remains in use. Courage, good brother! Even should you be ridiculed, no bones will be broken ; and if you are brave enough to despise contempt, even your sleep will not be disturbed.

Ishmael's mocking Isaac is only one among ten thousand proofs of the enmity which exists between the seed of the woman and the seed of the serpent. The mixture of these two in Abraham's household came about through his going down into Egypt and acting in an unbelieving manner towards Pharaoh. Then the Egyptian bondwoman was given to Sarah, and the evil element came into the camp. Sarah, in an evil hour, gave the bondwoman to her husband ;

hence ten thousand tears. No association of the unregenerate with the Church of God will avail to alter their nature: an Ishmael in Abraham's encampment is Ishmael still. To-day, the fiercest enemies of the truth of God are the aliens in our communion. These are they who make believers in sound evangelical teaching look like strangers in the Churches which were founded on the basis of scriptural doctrine. They make us foreigners in our own land. They are lenient to all manner of heresy; but the believer in the doctrines of grace they sneer at as old-fashioned and bigoted—a belated mortal who ought studiously to seek out a grave and bury himself. Yet will the man who trusts his God and believes in his covenant, be able to survive all mockeries; for he counts the reproach of Christ greater riches than all the treasures of Egypt. It is by no means shameful to trust God: on the contrary it is a point of honour with good men to trust in Him who is faithful and true; and if they have to suffer for it they do so joyfully. Gird yourselves, therefore, with a holy courage, you who are learning through grace to live upon *the promise* of God by faith. Was not the great Head of the family despised and rejected of men? Must not the rest of the brotherhood be conformed to the First-born? If we are made partakers of Christ's sufferings, we shall be partakers of his glory; wherefore, let us take part and lot with the Crucified heir of all things.

The Parting

" Nevertheless what saith the scripture? Cast out the bondwoman and her son : for the son of the bondwoman shall not be heir with the son of the freewoman."—Gal. iv. 30.

ISAAC and Ishmael lived together for a time. The self-religionist and the believer in the promise may be members of the same church for years, but they are not agreed, and cannot be happy together, for their principles are essentially opposed. As the believer grows in grace and enters upon his spiritual manhood, he will be more and more disagreeable to the legalist, and it will ultimately be seen that the two have no fellowship with one another. They must separate, and this is the word that will be fulfilled to the Ishmaelite : " Cast out this bondwoman and her son : for the son of this bondwoman shall not be heir with my son, even with Isaac." Grievous as the parting may be, it will be according to the divine will, and according to the necessities of the case. Oil and water will not mingle, neither will the natural man's religion agree with that which is born of *the promise*, and sustained by the promise. Their parting will be only the outward result of a serious difference which always existed.

Ishmael was sent away, but he soon ceased to regret it; for he found greater freedom with the wild tribes of the country, among whom he soon became a great man. He prospered much, and became the father of princes. He was in his proper sphere in the wide world ; there he had honour and gained a name among its great ones. Often it happens that the carnally religious man has many excellent habits and ways about him ; and having a desire to shine, he goes into society, and is appreciated and becomes notable. The world is sure to love its own. The aspiring religionist usually forsakes his first friends, and openly declares, " I have given up the old-fashioned style of religion. The saints were all very well while I was poor, but now I have made a fortune I feel that I must mix with a more fashionable set of people." He does so, and has his reward. Ishmael had his portion in this life, and never expressed a desire to share in the heavenly covenant and its mysterious blessings. If my reader would feel freer and more at home in society than in the church of God, let him know assuredly that he belongs to the world, and let him not deceive himself. As his heart is, such is he. No measure of force-work can turn Ishmael into Isaac, or a worldling into an heir of heaven.

Outwardly, and in this present life, the heir of the promise did not appear to have the best of it. Nor, indeed, should this be expected, since they who choose their heritage in the future have, in fact, agreed to accept trial in the present.

Isaac experienced certain afflictions which Ishmael never knew : he was mocked, and he was at last laid on the altar ; but nothing of the sort happened to Ishmael. You, who like Isaac are the children of the promise, must not envy those who are the heirs of this present life, though their lot seems easier than your own. Your temptation is to do so ; even as the Psalmist did when he was grieved because of the prosperity of the wicked. There is in this fretting a measure of running back from our spiritual choice: have we not agreed to take our part in the future rather than in the present? Do we rue the bargain ? Moreover, how absurd it is to envy those who are themselves so much to be pitied ! To lose the promise is practically to lose everything; and the self-righteous have lost it. These worldly professors have no spiritual light or life, and they desire none. What a loss, to be in the dark and not to know it! They have enough religion to make them respectable among men, and comfortable in their own consciences; but this is a sorry gain if they are abominable in the sight of God. They feel no inward fightings and wrestlings ; they find no contention of the old man against the new; and so they go through life with a jaunty air, knowing nothing till their end come. What wretchedness to be so besotted! Again, I say, do not envy them. Better far is the life of Isaac with its sacrifice, than that of Ishmael with its sovereignty and wild freedom ; for all the worldling's greatness will soon be ended and leave nothing behind it but that which will make the eternal world to be the more miserable.

Yet dream not that believers are unhappy. If in this life only we had hope we should be miserable indeed ; but *the promise* lights up our whole career, and makes us truly blessed. God's smile beheld by faith gives us fulness of joy. Put the believer's life at the greatest possible disadvantage, paint it in the darkest colours, take away from it not only comforts but necessaries, and even then the Christian at his worst is better than the worldling at his best. Let Ishmael have the whole world; ay, give him as many worlds as there are stars in the midnight sky, and we will not envy him. It is ours still to take up our cross, and to be strangers and foreigners with God in this land, as all our fathers were; for the promise, though it seems far off to others, we do, by faith, realize, and embrace, and in it we find a heaven below. Abiding with God, and with his people, we count our lot far better than that of the greatest and most honoured of the children of this world. The prospect of our Lord's second coming, and of our own eternal glory in fellowship with him, suffices to fill us with content while we wait for his appearing.

This difference on earth will lead to a sad division in death. The child of the bondwoman must be cast out in eternity as well as in time. None can enter heaven who claim it by their own doings, or boast that they have won it by their own strength. Glory is reserved for those who are saved by grace, and none who trust in self can enter there. What a terrible thing it will be when those who laboured to establish their own righteousness, and would not submit to the righteousness of Christ, shall be driven out! How will they then envy those lowly ones who were fain to accept pardon through the blood of Jesus! How will they discover their folly and wickedness in having despised the gift of God by preferring their own righteousness to that of the Son of God!

As the persons who are represented by Ishmael and Isaac are ultimately parted, so the principles upon which they rest must never be mingled, for they can by no means be made to agree. We cannot be saved in part by self, and in part by the promise of God. The principle and notion of earning salvation must be expelled from the mind. Every degree and form of it must be "cast out." If we are so unwise as to place our dependence partly on grace and partly on merit, we shall be resting one foot on a rock and the other on the sea, and our fall will be certain. There can be no dividing of the work or of the glory of salvation. It must be all of grace or all of works, all of God or all of man; but it cannot be half of one and half of the other. Cease from the vain attempt to unite two principles which are as adverse as fire and water. *The promise*, and the promise alone, must be the foundation of our hope, and all legal notions must be sternly dismissed as irreconcilable with salvation by grace. We must not begin in the spirit, and hope to be made perfect in the flesh. Our religion must be all of a piece. To sow with mingled seed, or to wear a garment of linen and woollen mixed, was forbidden to the Lord's ancient people; and to us it is unlawful to mingle mercy and merit, grace and debt. Whenever the notion of salvation by merit, or feeling, or ceremonies comes in, we must cast it out without delay, though it be as dear to us as Ishmael was to Abraham. Faith is not sight; the spirit is not the flesh; grace is not merit; and we must never forget the distinction, lest we fall into grievous error and miss the heritage which belongs only to the heirs according to promise.

Here is our confession of faith :—

"*Knowing that a man is not justified by the works of the law, but by the faith of Jesus Christ, even we have believed in Jesus Christ, that we might be justified by the faith of Christ, and not by the works of the law: for by the works of the law shall no flesh be justified.*—Gal. ii. 16.

Here also is the clear line of distinction as to the method of our salvation, and we desire to keep it plain and manifest :—

"*Even so then at this present time also there is a remnant according to the election of grace. And if by grace, then is it no more of works: otherwise grace is no more grace. But if it be of works, then is it no more grace: otherwise work is no more work.*"— Rom. xi. 5, 6.

Reader, do you see this?

Whose Are the Promises?

THE Lord is ever just and good towards his creatures : it is his nature so to be. But there was no necessity either in his justice or in his goodness that he should make promises of grace to those who had rebelled against him. Man has forfeited every form of claim upon his Maker, which he may have thought he had ; for he has broken the pure and holy law which he was under bond to have obeyed. Nothing is now due to man but the reward of his sins. If God should now deal with man upon the ground of strict justice he must condemn and punish him. Anything in the way of favour to a guilty creature must proceed only from the undeserved mercy and sovereign goodness of God : it must spring spontaneously from the goodwill and pleasure of the Most High. *The promises* of grace flow from the boundless love of God, and from that alone. They could not have proceeded from any other source. No single one of the race of man has any natural right to promises of blessing, nor can the whole world of men deserve them. God has made promises to men of his own free will and good pleasure, from no motive but that love which lies within himself.

He has chosen to make his promises to elect persons, who in process of time are discovered by their exercising faith in him. Those whom God has

chosen are led by the Holy Spirit to choose God
and his way of salvation by faith in Christ Jesus.
Those of the elect that come to years of discretion
are led to faith in Jesus; and all who have faith
in him may conclude beyond doubt that they are
of the chosen number to whom the promises are
given. To those who live and die in unbelief there
is no absolute and personal promise of God : they
are not under grace but under law, and to them
belong the threatenings and not the promises. These
prefer another method of dealing to that of gracious
promise, and in the end they perish as the result of
their foolish preference. The chosen of the Lord
are led to relinquish the proud way of self and
merit : they take to the road of faith, and so
find rest unto their souls. To believe the word of
God, and to trust in him whom God has sent to be
our Saviour may seem a small thing ; but indeed it
is not so : it is the sign of election, the token of
regeneration, the mark of coming glory. So to
believe that God is true as to rest one's eternal
interests upon his promise, bespeaks a heart
reconciled to God, a spirit in which the germ of
perfect holiness is present.

When we believe God as he is revealed in Christ
Jesus, we believe all *his promises*. Confidence in
the Person involves confidence in all that he speaks :
hence we accept all the promises of God as being
sure and certain. We do not trust one promise and
doubt another, but we rely upon each one as true,
and we believe it to be true *to us* so far as it has
respect to our condition and circumstances. We

argue from general statements to particular applications.   He who has said that he will save those
who believe in him will save *me* since I believe in
him ; and every blessing which he has engaged to
bestow upon believers he will bestow upon *me* as a
believer.   This is sound reasoning, and by it we
justify the faith by which we live and are comforted.
Not because *I* deserve anything, but because God
has freely promised it to me in Christ Jesus, therefore I shall receive it : this is the reason and ground
of our hope.

One wonders at first sight that all men do not
believe God.   It would seem as if this mark of
divine election would be universally present; for
God cannot lie, and there is no reason to suspect
him of change, or failure of ability to keep his word.
Yet, so false is the heart of man, that man doubts
his Maker.   He hates his God, and therefore
disbelieves him.   It is the surest proof of man's
natural enmity against God that he dares to impute
falsehood to one who is truth itself.   " He that
believeth not God hath made him a liar; because he
believeth not the record that God gave of his Son "
(1 John v. 10).

Real, practical trust in the living God, easy as it
seems to be, is a virtue which was never practised by
an unrenewed heart.   The glorious atonement made
by the incarnate Son of God is worthy of the
reliance of all mankind.   One would have imagined
that every sinner would have washed at once in
this cleansing fountain, and without hesitation
would have believed in the divine Redeemer : but

it is very far from being so. Men will not come
unto Christ that they may have life. They would
rather trust in anything than in the sacrifice of
Jesus. Until the Holy Ghost works a miracle upon
a man, he will not confide in the great sacrifice
which God has provided and accepted for the
putting away of guilt. Hence it is that this simple,
common-place matter of faith, yet becomes the
distinguishing mark of the chosen of the Lord. No
other token is so infallible: "He that believeth on
him hath everlasting life." Feelings and actions
may all serve as evidences; but the master evidence
of an interest in the promise of God is faith in him.
"Abraham believed God, and it was counted to
him for righteousness": there were many other
good points in the patriarch's character, but this
was the decisive one,—he believed God; indeed,
this was the root of all else that was commendable
in him.

Worldly-wise men despise faith, and set it in
contrast with virtuous action; but this contrast is
not fair: one might as well contrast a fountain with
its stream, or the sun with its own heat. If true
faith be the mother of holiness, let the mother grace
have praise because of its offspring, and let it not
be contrasted therewith. Such unfair reasoning
comes of wanton malice: if men loved good works
as much as they pretend to do, they would love
the faith which produces them.

God loves faith because it honours him, and also
because it leads to acts of obedience to him, which
obedience includes love to our fellow-men. There

is more in faith than meets the eye. It is in one
aspect the greatest of all good works, even as our
Lord Jesus teaches us. The Jews said to him
(John vi. 28, 29), "What shall we do, that we might
work the works of God?" They would fain perform godlike works, works above all others approved
of the Lord. Jesus answered them, "This is the
work of God, that ye believe on him whom he hath
sent." As much as to say—the most divinely
approved work possible to you, is to believe in the
Messiah. To trust in the Lord Jesus is the climax
of virtue. Proud men may sneer, but this statement
is true. "Without faith it is impossible to please
God;" but "he that believeth in him is not condemned." *The promise* is made to him that
believes the promise, and to him it shall be fulfilled.
He who embraces the promise is embraced by the
promise. He who accepts Christ is accepted in
Christ. He who truly believes is surely saved.

READER, DO YOU BELIEVE YOUR GOD?

The Promise a Free Gift

"Whereby are given unto us exceeding great and precious promises."—2 Peter i. 4.

OBSERVE that word "*given.*" Peter says, "Whereby *are given* unto us exceeding great and precious promises." We are beholden for everything to the gift of God. We live upon divine charity. All that we have we have received as a gift, and all we are to have must come in the same way. "The wages of sin is death, but the *gift* of God is eternal life." We are unable to earn anything, but God is able to give all things. Salvation must be all a gift, a free gift, an undeserved gift, a spontaneous gift of divine love. *The promise* of salvation is of the same nature.

"It is more blessed to give than to receive"; and he that is most blest of all, the ever-blessed God, delights to give. It is as much his nature to give as it is the nature of the sun to shine, or of a river to flow. How blessed we are in being receivers! This is emphasized greatly, when we reflect how necessary it is that we should receive; for the things that we need are such that if we do not obtain them we are lost now, and lost for ever. We are without life, without light, without hope, and without peace, if we are without God. If God does not give to us according to the riches of his grace, we are then worse than naked, and poor, and miserable; we are

utterly and altogether undone. It is not possible
that we should deserve such rich gifts. Even if we
could deserve anything, these must come to us
without money and without price. A promise from
God must be a boon of grace : we cannot claim that
God should promise us his favour, and the priceless
boons which are wrapped up in it.

This teaches us what posture to take up. Pride
ill becomes dependants. He who lives upon gifts
should be humble and grateful. We are beggars at
the door of mercy. At the beautiful gate of the
temple we sit down every day to ask an alms, not
of the worshippers, but of him whom angels worship.
As often as our Lord passes by, we ask and he gives ;
nor are we surprised that we receive from his love ;
for he has promised to bestow great mercies. He
taught us to say, "Give us this day our daily bread,"
and therefore we are neither ashamed nor afraid
to ask all things from him. Ours is a life of
dependence, and we delight to have it so. It is
sweet to take all things from the hands of our
crucified Lord. Happy is the poverty which leads
us to be rich in Christ. We earn nothing, and yet
receive everything, thrice blest in being hourly
partakers of the gift of God. "Whereby are *given*
unto us exceeding great and precious promises."

Beloved, this teaching as to *the promise* coming
of pure gift should be exceedingly encouraging to
all who feel their lost estate, and own that they are
spiritually bankrupt. To such it is a word of good
cheer, that everything is freely *given* to us of God :
why should he not give to them as well as to other

needy ones? Those of us who rejoice in God have
received all things as a free gift; why should not
others receive the like? They say, "There is nothing
freer than a gift": why should not my reader
receive as well as myself? To one who is willing
to give, poverty, on the part of the receiver, is a
recommendation instead of an obstacle. Come,
then, you who are without merit, Christ will be
your merit. Come, you that have no righteousness,
he will be your righteousness. Come, you who are
as full of sin as an egg is full of meat, and the
pardoning Lord will put away your sin. Come,
you who are utterly forlorn, and be made rich in
Jesus. The trade of a mendicant will suit you, and
you will prosper in it; for I see you have a cruel
hunger, and an empty wallet. He that cannot dig
should not be ashamed to beg. A beggar needs
no stock-in-trade. "Old shoes and clouted," rags
worn and foul—these form a fit livery for a beggar.
Are you not dressed in this fashion spiritually?
The poorer the wretch, the more welcome is he at
the door of divine charity. The less you have of
your own, the more welcome you are to him who
giveth freely and upbraideth not.

> "Come, ye needy, come and welcome,
>   God's free bounty glorify;
> True belief, and true repentance,
>   Every grace that brings us nigh,
>   Without money,
>   Come to Jesus Christ and buy."

Yes, it is all a gift. This is the gospel that we
are sent to preach to you—"God so loved the world

that he *gave* his only begotten Son, that whosoever believeth in him should not perish, but have everlasting life." "This is the record, that God hath *given* to us eternal life, and this life is in his Son" (1 John v. 11). On God's part it is all giving; on our part it is all receiving. *The promise* is already made, and freely made : it will be fulfilled, and freely fulfilled. God does not begin with giving, and then go on to charging a price. No commission is payable upon receipt of his grace. He does not ask or receive a farthing; his love is altogether a gift. As a gift you may accept his promise : he will not degrade himself by listening to any other terms.

The word given in the text is a plain invitation to the poorest of the poor. Oh that they would make bold to avail themselves of it! The great bell is ringing, ringing that all who will to come to the great table of infinite liberality may hear it and draw near. Freely, according to the riches of his grace, doth God promise salvation and eternal life to all who believe on his Son, Jesus Christ. His promise is firm and sure, why is it that men do not believe it?

Reader, what say you to the promise so freely given to all believers? Will you believe it and live thereby?

The Promise of God a Reality

SURELY it is a wonderful thing that the eternal God should make promises to his own creatures. Before he pledged his word he was free to do as it pleased him; but after he has made a promise, his truth and honour bind him to do as he has said. To him, indeed, this is no limiting of his liberty; for the promise is always the declaration of his sovereign will and good pleasure, and it is ever his delight to act according to his word : yet is it marvellous condescension for the free spirit of the Lord to form for itself covenant bonds. Yet he hath done so. The Lord has made a covenant of grace with men, in which he has confirmed his promises, not only by pledging his word, but by giving his oath; "that by two immutable things in which it was impossible for God to lie, we might have strong consolation who have fled for refuge to lay hold upon the hope set before us."

In that covenant there are promises many and precious, all confirmed in Christ Jesus, and established for ever upon the foundation of divine truthfulness. This is our hope, even as Paul wrote to Titus : "In hope of eternal life, which God, that cannot lie, promised before the world began."

God has promised, and on the faithfulness of
that promise we build our confidence for time and
for eternity. We think it no imprudent thing to
rest our soul's salvation upon the promise of our
faithful Creator. To help us so to trust, the promises were not only spoken but written. Men say
they like to have an agreement in black and white,
and we have it so in this case. " In the volume
of the book it is written." In the page of inspiration the record stands ; and as we believe our
Bibles, we are bound to rely upon the promises
contained therein.

It is a cause of much weakness to many that
they do not treat *the promises* of God as realities.
If a friend makes them a promise, they regard it
as a substantial thing, and look for that which
it secures ; but the declarations of God are often
viewed as so many words which mean very little.
This is most dishonouring to the Lord, and very
injurious to ourselves. Rest assured that the Lord
never trifles with words : " Hath he said, and will
he not do it ? " His engagements are always kept.
David said of the Lord's promises to him, " Yet
hast thou made with me an everlasting covenant,
ordered in all things and sure." God speaks
deliberately, in due order and determination, and
we may depend upon it that his words are sure, and
will be fulfilled as certainly as they are uttered.
Have any who have trusted in the Lord been
confounded ? Can an instance be found in which
our God has been false to his word ? The ages
cannot produce a single proof that the promise-

making Jehovah has run back from that which he has spoken.

We admire fidelity in men, and we cannot imagine it to be absent from the character of God, and therefore we may safely reckon upon his being as good as his word. It is said of Blücher, that when he was marching to help Wellington at Waterloo, his troops faltered. "It can't be done," said they. "It *must* be done," was his answer. "I have promised to be there—*promised*, do you hear? You would not have me break my word." He was at Waterloo to good purpose: he would not be hindered, for his promise was given. We praise such faithfulness; we should think little of one who did not exhibit it. Shall the Lord God Almighty fail in his promise? No, he will move heaven and earth, and shake the universe, rather than be behind-hand with his word. He seems to say—"It must be done. I have promised—promised, do you hear?" Sooner than his promise should fail, he spared not his own Son. Better Jesus die than the word of the Lord be broken. I say again,— depend upon it, the Lord means what he says, and will make good every syllable. Yet none but the chosen seed will believe him. *Reader*, will you?

God must be true, whoever else may deceive. If all the truth in the whole world could be gathered together, it would be but as a drop in the bucket compared with the truthfulness of God. The veracity of the most just of men is vanity itself compared with the sure truth of God. The faithfulness of the most upright of men is as a vapour,

but the faithfulness of God is as a rock.   If we
trust in good men we ought infinitely more to trust
in the good God.   Why does it seem a singular
thing to rest on the promise of God ?   Somehow it
looks to many to be a dreamy, sentimental, mystical
business ;   and yet if we view it calmly it is the
most matter of fact transaction that can be.   God
is real : all else is shadowy.   He is certain : all else
is questionable.   He must keep his word, this is an
absolute necessity : how else could he be God ?   To
believe God should be an act of the mind which
needs no effort.   Even if difficulties could be
suggested, the simple and pure in heart should
spontaneously say, " Let God be true and every
man a liar."   To give God less than an implicit
faith is to rob him of an honour justly due to his
spotless holiness.

Our duty to God demands that we accept his
promise, and act upon it.   Every honest man has a
right to credence, and much more does the God of
truth deserve it.   We ought to treat the promise as
in itself the substance of the thing promised, just
as we look upon a man's cheque or note of hand as
an actual payment.   Promises to pay are passed
from hand to hand in daily business, as if they
were current money of the merchant ; and God's
promises should be regarded in the same light.
Let us believe that we have the petitions which
we have asked of him.   He warrants our so doing,
and promises to reward such faith.

Let us regard the promise as a thing so sure and
certain that we act upon it, and make it to be a

chief figure in all our calculations. The Lord promises eternal life to those who believe in Jesus; therefore, if we really believe in Jesus, let us conclude that we have eternal life, and rejoice in the great privilege. The promise of God is our best ground of assurance; it is far more sure than dreams and visions, and fancied revelations; and it is far more to be trusted than feelings, either of joy or sorrow. It is written, "He that believeth in him is not condemned." I believe in Jesus, therefore I am not condemned. This is good reasoning, and the conclusion is certain. If God has said so, it is so, beyond all doubt. Nothing can be more certain than that which is declared by God himself; nothing more sure to happen, than that which he has guaranteed by his own hand and seal.

When a soul is under conviction, it perceives *the threatenings* of the Lord with an intensity of belief which is very noticeable, since its awe-stricken faith breeds within the heart overwhelming terror and dismay. Why should not *the promises* be accepted with a similar realization? Why not accepted with the same certainty? If it be made true in the conscience that he that believeth not shall be damned, it may be accepted with equal assurance, that he that believeth and is baptized shall be saved, since the latter is as much the word of God as the former. The tendency of the awakened mind, is to dwell upon the dark side of God's word, and feel the full force of it; and at the same time to neglect the brighter portion of the record, and cast a doubt upon it, as though it were too

good to be true. This is folly. Every blessing is
too good for us to receive if we measure it by our
unworthiness; but no blessing is too good for
God to give, if we judge of it by his surpassing
excellence. It is after the nature of a God of love
to give boundless blessing. If Alexander gave
like a king, shall not Jehovah give like a God?

We have sometimes heard persons say, "As sure
as death"; we suggest that we might as fitly say,
"As sure as life." Gracious things are as sure as
"terrible things in righteousness." "Whosoever
believeth in Jesus shall not perish, but have everlasting life." It must be so, for God's word hath
said it, and there can be no mistake about it.

Yes, the Lord means what he says. He never
mocks men with barren words and empty sounds.
Why should he deceive his creatures, and ask from
them a barren confidence? The Lord may go
beyond his word in giving more than it might be
thought to mean; but he can never fall short of it.
We may interpret his promises upon the most
liberal scale. He never falls below the largest
rendering which expectation can give to the
promise. Faith never yet outstripped the bounty
of the Lord. Let us embrace the promise, and
rejoice that it is substance and not shadow. Let
us even now rejoice in it as being the reality of
that for which we are hoping.

The Peculiar Treasure of Believers

GOD'S promises are the peculiar treasure of believers: the substance of faith's heritage lies in them. All the promises of our covenant God are ours to have and to hold as our personal possession. By faith we receive and embrace them, and they constitute our true riches. We have certain most precious things in actual enjoyment at this present; but the capital of our wealth, the bulk of our estate lies in *the promise* of our God. That which we have in hand is only the earnest penny of the immeasurable wage of grace which is to be paid to us in due time.

The Lord graciously gives us even now all things necessary for this life and godliness; but his choicest blessings are held in reserve for time to come. Grace given to us from day to day is our spending money for travelling expenses on the road home; but it is not our estate. Providential supplies are rations on the march, but not the ultimate feast of love. We may miss these wayside meals, but we are bound for The Supper of The Lamb. Thieves may rob us of our ready cash; but our peculiar treasure is hid with Christ in God beyond all fear of loss. The hand which bled to make this treasure ours is keeping it for us.

It is a great joy to have a full assurance of our interest in the promises : but this joyful feeling we may lose, and we may find it hard to get it again, and yet the eternal inheritance will be quite as truly ours. It is as though a man should have in his hand a fair copy of his title-deeds, and should much delight himself in reading it until by some mischance his copy is stolen or mislaid. The loss of his writings is not the loss of his rights. His comfortable reading of the title-deed is suspended, but his claim to his property is not shaken. The covenant promise is entailed upon every joint-heir with Christ, and there is no such thing as the breaking of this entail. Many an event may tend to shake the believer's sense of security, but "the promise is sure to all the seed." Our greatest possession lies not in any present comfort or confidence which we receive from the promise, but in *the promise* itself, and in the glorious heritage which it secures to us. Our inheritance lies not on this side Jordan. Our city of habitation is not within the borders of the present : we see it from afar, but we wait for its full enjoyment in that illustrious day when our covenant Head shall be revealed in his glory, and all his people with him. God's providence is our earthly pension ; but God's *promise* is our heavenly heritage.

Did it ever occur to you to enquire why the way of God's dealing with his chosen should be by promises ? He could have bestowed his blessings at once, and without giving us notice of his intention. In this way he would have obviated the necessity of a

covenant concerning them.   There was no necessity
in the nature of things for this plan of promising.
The Lord might have given us all the mercies we
needed, without pledging himself to do so.   God,
with his great strength of will, and firmness of
purpose, could have secretly resolved in himself to
do all that he does unto believers without having
made them the confidants of his divine counsels.
Many a decree hath he kept secret from the foundations of the world ; why, then, hath he revealed
his purposes of blessing?   Why is it that his
dealings with his people from the gate of Eden
till now have been upon the footing of publicly
expressed promises ?

Does not the question answer itself?   In the
first place, *we could not have been believers if there
had not been a promise in which to believe.*   If the
system of salvation is to be by faith, a promise
must be made upon which faith can exercise
itself.   The plan of salvation by faith is selected
because it is most suitable to the principle of
grace ; and this involves the giving of promises,
that faith may have both food and foundation.
Faith without a promise would be a foot without
ground to stand upon ; and such a faith, if faith it
could be called, would be unworthy of the plan of
grace.   Faith being chosen as the great evangelical
command, the promise becomes an essential part of
the gospel dispensation.

Moreover, it is a charming thought that *our
good God designedly gives us promises of good things
that we may enjoy them twice; first by faith, and*

then by fruition. He gives twice by giving by
promise ; and we also receive twice in embracing
the promise by faith. The time for the fulfilment
of many a promise is not by-and-by ; but by
faith we realize the promise, and the foreshadow-
ing of the expected blessing fills our souls with
the benefit long before it actually comes. We
have an instance of this upon a large scale in
Old Testament saints. The great promise of the
seed in whom the nations should be blessed was
the ground of faith, the foundation of hope, and
the cause of salvation to thousands of believers
before the Son of God actually appeared among
men. Did not our Lord say, " Abraham saw my
day : he saw it, and was glad " ? The great father
of the faithful saw the day of Christ through the
telescope of God's promise, by the eye of faith ;
and though Abraham did not obtain the fulfilment
of that promise, but fell asleep before the coming
of the Lord, as did Isaac, and Jacob, and many
others of the saints, yet he had Christ to trust
in, Christ to rejoice in, and Christ to love and serve.
Before he was born in Bethlehem, or offered upon
Calvary, Jesus was so seen of the faithful as to
make them glad. The promise gave them a Saviour
before the Saviour actually appeared. So is it with
us at this time : by means of the promise we enter
into possession of things not seen as yet. By
anticipation we make the coming blessing present
to us. Faith obliterates time, annihilates distance,
and brings future things at once into its possession, The Lord has not as yet given us to join the

hallelujahs of heaven: we have not yet passed
through the gates of pearl, nor have we trodden the
streets of transparent gold; but the promise of
such felicity lights up the gloom of our affliction,
and yields us immediate foretastes of glory. We
triumph by faith before our hands actually grasp
the palm. We reign with Christ by faith before
our heads are encircled with our unfading coronets.
Many and many a time we have seen the dawn of
heaven while we have beheld light breaking from
the promise. When faith has been vigorous we
have climbed where Moses stood and gazed upon
the land which floweth with milk and honey; and
then, when Atheist has declared that there is
no Celestial City, we have answered, " Did we not
see it from the Delectable Mountains?" We have
seen enough by means of the promise to make
us quite sure of the glory which the Lord hath
prepared for them that love him; and thus we
have obtained our first draught of the promised
bliss, and found therein a sure pledge of our
full and final enjoyment of it.

Do you not think that the promise also is intended *to lead us constantly away from the things
that are seen, onward and upward to the spiritual
and the unseen?* The man who lives on the
promise of God has risen into quite another atmosphere than that which oppresses us in these low-
lying vales of daily life. " It is better," says one,
" to trust in the Lord than to put confidence in
men. It is better to trust in the Lord than to put
confidence in princes." And so, indeed, it is; for

it is more spiritual, more noble, more inspiring.
We need to be raised to this elevated trust by divine
power; for our soul naturally cleaveth unto the
dust. Alas! we are hampered by our idolatrous
desire to see, and touch, and handle: we trust our
senses, but have not sense enough to trust our God.
The same spirit which led Israel to cry in the
wilderness, "Make us gods to go before us," leads
us to sigh for something tangible by flesh and blood,
whereon our confidence may take hold. We hunger for proofs, tokens, and evidences, and will not
accept the divine promise as better and surer than
all visible signs. Thus we pine away in hungering
for tokens and evidences which are visible, till we
are driven to try the better and surer things which
are invisible. Oh, it is a blessed thing for a child
of God to be made to quit the sand of things temporal for the rock of things eternal, by being called
upon to walk by the rule of the promise!

Furthermore, *the promises are to our hearts a
help to the realization of the Lord himself.* The
child of God, when he believes the promise, is
brought to feel that God is, and that he is the
rewarder of them that diligently seek him. Our
tendency is to get away from a real God. We
live and move in the region of materialism, and we
are apt to be enthralled by its influences. We feel
these bodies to be real when we have pain in
them, and this world to be real when we are
weighted with its crosses: yet the body is a poor
tent, and the world a mere bubble. These visible
things are unsubstantial, but they appear sadly

solid to us: what we need is to know the invisible
to be quite as real as that which is seen, and even
more so. We need a living God in this dying
world, and we must have him truly near us, or
we shall fail. The Lord is training his people to
perceive himself: the promise is part of this educa-
tional process.

When the Lord gives us faith, and we rest on his
promise, then are we brought face to face with him.
We ask, "Who gave this promise? Who is to
fulfil this promise?" and our thoughts are thus led
into the presence of the glorious Jehovah. We
feel how necessary he is to the whole system of our
spiritual life; and how truly he enters into it, so
that in him we live, and move, and have our being.
If the promise cheers us, it is only because there is
God at the back of it; for the mere words of the
promise are nothing to us except as they come
from the lips of God who cannot lie, and except
as they are wrought out by that hand which cannot
fail. The promise is the forecast of the divine
purpose, the shadow of the coming blessing; in
fact, it is the token of God's own nearness to us.
We are cast upon God for the fulfilment of his engagements, and that is one of his reasons for dealing
with us after the method of promise. Perhaps if
the Lord had dropped our mercies at our door
without a previous hint of their coming, we should
not have cared to know whence they came. If
he had sent them with unbroken regularity, even as
he makes his sun to rise every morning, we might
have slighted them as common results of natural

laws, and so have forgotten God because of the
punctuality of his providence. Certainly we should
have lacked that grand test of the being and loving-
kindness of God which we now receive as we read
the promise, accept it by faith, plead it in prayer,
and in due season see it fulfilled.

That regularity of divine bounty which ought
to sustain and increase faith is often the means of
weakening it. He whose bread comes to him by a
government annuity or a quarterly rent, is tempted
to forget that God has any hand in it. It ought
not to be so; but through the hardness of our
hearts such an ill result does frequently follow from
the constancy of a gracious providence.

I should not wonder if those Israelites who were
born in the wilderness, and had gathered manna
every morning for years, had also ceased to wonder
at it, or to see the hand of the Lord in it. Shameful
stupidity! but, ah, how common! Many a person
has lived from hand to mouth, and seen the hand
of the Lord in the gift of every morsel of bread:
at last by God's goodness he has prospered in this
world, and obtained a regular income, which he has
received without care and trouble, and shortly he
has come to look at it as the natural result of his
own industry, and has no longer praised the loving-
kindness of the Lord. To be living without the
conscious presence of the Lord is a horrible state
of affairs. Supplied, but not by God! Sustained
without the hand of God! It were better to be
poor, or sick, or exiled, and thus to be driven to
approach our heavenly Father. To avoid our

coming under the curse of forgetting God, the Lord is pleased to put his choicest blessings into connection with his own promises, and to call forth our faith in reference to them. He will not allow his mercies to become veils to hide his face from the eyes of our love; but he makes them windows through which he looks upon us. The Promiser is seen in the promise, and we watch to see his hand in the performance ; thus are we saved from that natural atheism which lurks within the heart of man.

I think it well to repeat that *we are put under the régime of promise in order that we may grow in faith*. How could there be faith without a promise ? How growing faith without grasping more and more of the promise ? We are made to remember in the hour of need, that God has said, " Call upon me in the day of trouble, and I will deliver thee." Faith believes this word, calls upon God, and finds herself delivered : thus she is strengthened, and made to glorify the Lord.

Sometimes faith does not find the promise fulfilled at the moment ; but she has to wait a while. This is fine exercise for her, and serves to test her sincerity and force : this test brings assurance to the believer, and fills him with comfort. By-and-by the answer is given to prayer, the promised boon is bestowed, faith is crowned with victory, and glory is given to God ; but meanwhile the delay has produced the patience of hope, and made every mercy to wear a double value. Promises afford training-ground for faith : these are poles

and leaping-bars for the athletic exercise of our
young faith, by the use of which it grows to be so
strong that it can break through a troop, or leap
over a wall. When our confidence in God is firm
we laugh at impossibility, and cry, "It shall be
done"; but this could not be if there were not an
infallible promise wherewith faith could gird itself.

*Those promises which as yet are unfulfilled are
precious helps to our advance in the spiritual life.*
We are encouraged by exceeding great and precious
promises to aspire to higher things. The prospect
of good things to come strengthens us to endure,
and to press forward. You and I are like little
children who are learning to walk, and are induced
to take step after step by an apple being held out
to them. We are persuaded to try the trembling
legs of our faith by the sight of a promise. Thus we
are drawn to go a step nearer to our God. The
little one is very apt to cling to a chair, it is hard
to get it to quit all hold, and venture upon its feet;
but at last it becomes daring enough for a tiny trip,
which it ends at its mother's knees. This little
venture leads to another and another, till it runs
alone. The apple plays a great part in the
training of the babe, and so does the promise in the
education of faith. Promise after promise have
we received, till now, I trust, we can give up
crawling on the earth, and clinging to the things
which rest upon it, and can commit ourselves to
the walk of faith.

The promise is a needful instrument in the education of our souls in all manner of spiritual graces

and actions. How often have I said, " My Lord,
I have received much from thee, blessed be thy
name for it; but there is yet a promise more
which I have not enjoyed; therefore I will go
forward till I attain its fulfilment! The future is
an unknown country, but I enter it with thy
promise, and expect to find in it the same goodness
and mercy which have followed me hitherto; yea,
I look for greater things than these."

Nor must I forget to remind you, that *the
promise is part of the economy of our spiritual
condition here below because it excites prayer.*
What is prayer but the promise pleaded? A
promise is, so to speak, the raw material of prayer.
Prayer irrigates the fields of life with the waters
which are stored up in the reservoirs of promise.
The promise is the power of prayer. We go to
God, and we say to him, " Do as thou hast said.
O Lord, here is thy word; we beseech thee fulfil
it." Thus the promise is the bow by which we
shoot the arrows of supplication. I like in my
time of trouble to find a promise which exactly fits
my need, and then to put my finger on it, and
say, " Lord, this is thy word; I beseech thee to
prove that it is so, by carrying it out in my case.
I believe that this is thine own writing; and I
pray thee make it good to my faith." I believe in
plenary inspiration, and I humbly look to the Lord
for a plenary fulfilment of every sentence that he
has put on record. I delight to hold the Lord to
the very words that he has used, and to expect him
to do as he has said, because he has said it. It is

a great thing to be driven to prayer by necessity ;
but it is a better thing to be drawn to it by the
expectation which the promise arouses. Should
we pray at all if God did not find us an occasion
for praying, and then encourage us with gracious
promises of an answer? As it is, in the order of
providence we are tried, and then we try the
promises ; we are brought to spiritual hunger, and
then we are fed on the word which proceedeth out
of the mouth of God. By the system which the
Lord follows with his chosen we are kept in
constant intercourse with him, and are not allowed
to forget our heavenly Father : we are often at the
throne of grace, blessing God for promises fulfilled,
and pleading promises on which we rely. We
pay innumerable visits to the divine dwelling-
place, because there is a promise to plead, and a
God waiting to be gracious. Is not this an order
of things for which to be grateful? Ought we not
to magnify the Lord that he doth not pour upon
us showers of unpromised blessings, but he en-
hances the value of his benefits by making them
the subjects of his promises and the objects of
our faith?

The Valuation of the Promises

"Whereby are given unto us exceeding great and precious promises."—2 Peter i. 4.

WE have thought upon *the promises* as our treasure: it is time that we should take a survey of them, and calculate their value. Since the promises are our estate, let us form a correct estimate of our wealth: possibly we may not fully know how rich we are. It will be a pity to pine in poverty from ignorance of our large property. May the Holy Spirit help us to form a due valuation of the riches of grace and glory reserved for us in the covenant of promise!

The apostle Peter speaks of the promises as "*exceeding* great and precious." They do indeed exceed all things with which they can be compared. None ever promised as God has done. Kings have promised even to the half of their kingdoms; but what of that? God promised to give his own Son, and even his own Self, to his people; and he did it. Princes draw a line somewhere, but the Lord sets no bounds to the gifts which he ordains for his chosen.

The promises of God not only exceed all precedent, but they also exceed all imitation. Even with God himself for an example, none have been able to vie with him in the language of liberality. The promises of Jehovah are as much above all other promises as the heavens are above the earth.

They also exceed all expectation. He does for us "exceeding abundantly above all that we ask or even think." Nobody could have imagined that the Lord would have made such promises as he has made: they surpass the dreams of romance. Even the most sanguine hopes are left far behind, and the loftiest conceptions are outdone. The Bible must be true, for it could not have been invented: the promises contained in it are greater for quantity and better for quality than the most expectant could have looked for. God surprises us with the surpassing fulness of his cheering words: he overwhelms us with favours till, like David, we sit down in wonder, and cry, "Whence is this to me?"

The promises exceed all measurement: there is an abyss of depth in them as to meaning, a heaven of height in them as to excellence, and an ocean of breadth in them as to duration. We might say of every promise, "It is high: I cannot attain to it." As a whole, the promises exhibit the fulness and all-sufficiency of God: like God himself they fill all things. Unbounded in their range, they are everywhere about us, whether we wake or sleep, go forth or return. They cover the whole of life from the cradle to the tomb. A sort of omnipresence may be ascribed to them; for they surround us in all places, and at all times. They are our pillow when we fall asleep, and when we awake they are still with us. "How precious also are thy thoughts unto me, O God! How great is the sum of them!" "Exceeding" all conception and calculation; we admire them and adore their Giver, but we can never measure them.

The promises even exceed all experience. Those men of God who have known the Lord for fifty or sixty years have never yet extracted the whole of the marrow from his promise. Still it might be said, "the arrow is beyond thee." Somewhat better and deeper yet remains to be searched out in the future. He who dives deepest by experience into the depths of the divine promises is fully aware that there is yet a lower depth of grace and love unfathomable. The promise is longer than life, broader than sin, deeper than the grave, and higher than the clouds. He that is most acquainted with the golden book of promise is still a new beginner in its study: even the ancients of Israel find that this volume passeth knowledge.

Certainly I need not say that the promises exceed all expression. If all the tongues of men and of angels were given me, I could not tell you how great are the promises of God. They exceed not only one language, but all languages: they surpass the glowing praises of all the enthusiasts that have ever spoken. Even angels before the throne still desire to look into these marvels, for they cannot yet reach the mystery—the length, and breadth, and height. In Christ Jesus everything exceeds description; and the promises in him exhaust the force of all speech, human or divine. Vain is it for me to attempt the impossible.

Exceeding "*great*" Peter says they are; and he knew right well. They come from a great God, they assure us of great love, they come to great sinners, they work for us great results, and deal with great matters. They are as great as greatness itself; they bring us the great God, to be our God for ever and ever. God's first promise was that in which he engaged to give us his Son. We are wont to say, "Thanks be unto God for his unspeakable gift," but let not the words glide too easily over the tongue. For God to give his Only-begotten Son is beyond all conception a great deed of love: indeed, "great" seems too little a word to describe such a miracle of love. When the Lord had given his Son, freely delivering him up for us all—what then? He promised to give the Holy Ghost, the Comforter, to abide with us for ever. Can we measure the value of that great promise? The Holy Ghost came down at Pentecost, in fulfilment of that ancient prophecy: was not that marvellous descent an exceeding great and precious gift? Remember that the Holy Spirit works in us all those graces which prepare us for the society of heaven. Glory be to God for this visitation of boundless grace!

What next? Our Lord has given us now the promise that he will "come again a second time without a sin offering unto salvation." Can all the saints put together fully measure the greatness of the promise of the Second Advent? This means infinite felicity for saints. What else has he promised? Why, that because he lives we shall

live also. We shall possess an immortality of bliss
for our souls; we shall enjoy also a resurrection
for our bodies; we shall reign with Christ; we
shall be glorified at his right hand. Promises
fulfilled and promises unfulfilled, promises for time
and promises for eternity—they are indeed so
great that it is impossible to conceive of their
being greater.

> "What more can he say than to you he hath said?
> You who unto Jesus for refuge have fled."

O ye whose minds are trained to lofty thought,
tell me your estimate of the faithful promises! I
perceive a promise of the pardon of sin. O ye forgiven ones, declare the greatness of this boon!
There is the promise of adoption. Children of
God, you begin to know what manner of love the
Father hath bestowed on you in this; tell out
your joy! There is the promise of help in every
time of need. Tried ones, you know how the Lord
sustains and delivers his chosen; proclaim the
largeness of his grace! There is the promise that
as your day your strength shall be. You that are
working hard for Christ, or bearing his cross from
day to day, you feel how exceeding great is that
promise of sure support. What a word is this:
"No good thing will he withhold from them that
walk uprightly"! What a sentence is this: "All
things work together for good to them that love
God, to them who are the called according to his
purpose"! Who can estimate the breadth of
such a gracious assurance? No, you need not take

that foot-rule from your pocket : it will not serve
you here.   If you could take the distance of a
fixed star as your base, all reckoning would still be
impossible.   All the chains that ever measured the
acres of the wealthy are useless here.   A certain
millionaire glories that his estate reaches from sea
to sea ; but no ocean can bound the possessions
secured to us by the promise of our faithful God
The theme is so exceeding great that it exceeds
my power of expression, and therefore I forbear.

The verse, upon which we are now thinking,
speaks of "exceeding great *and precious promises.*"
Greatness and preciousness seldom go together ;
but in this instance they are united in an exceeding
degree.   When the Lord opens his mouth to make
a promise, it is sure to be worthy of him : he speaks
words of exceeding power and richness.   Instead
of trying to speak of the preciousness of the
promises doctrinally, I will fall back upon the
experience of those who have tried and proved
them.

Beloved, how precious the promises. are to the
poor and needy !   They that know their spiritual
poverty discern the value of the promise which
meets their case.   How precious, also, are the
promises, to those who have enjoyed the fulfilment
of them !   We can go back in memory to times
and seasons when we were brought low, and the
Lord helped us according to his word.   Even before
he brought us up out of the horrible pit, we were
kept from sinking in the deep mire by looking
forward to the time when he would appear for our

rescue. His promise kept us from dying of hunger long before we reached the feast of love. In the expectation of future trial our confidence is in the promise. Thus it is very precious to us even before it is actually fulfilled. The more we believe the promise, the more we find in it to believe. So precious is the word of the Lord to us, that we could part with everything we have rather than throw away a single sentence of it. We cannot tell which promise of the Lord we may next need : that which we have hardly noticed may yet turn out at a certain moment to be essential to our life. Thank God, we are not called to part with any one of the jewels from the breastplate of Holy Scripture : they are all yea and amen in Christ Jesus to the glory of God by us !

How precious are the promises when we lie sick, gazing into eternity by the month together, sorely tried and tempted through pain and weariness ! All depressing circumstances lose their power for evil when our faith takes firm hold upon the promises of God. How sweet to feel I have my head on the promise, and my heart on the promise : I rest on the truth of the Most High ! Not on earthly vanity, but on heavenly verity, do I repose. There is nothing to be found elsewhere comparable to this perfect rest. The pearl of peace is found among the precious promises. That is precious indeed which can support dying men, and cause them to pass into eternity with as much delight as if they were going to a marriage-feast. That which lasts for ever, and lasts good for ever,

is most precious. That which brings all things
with it, and hath all things in it,—that is precious
indeed ; and such is the promise of God.

If such be the greatness and preciousness of the
promises, *let us joyfully accept and believe them.*
Shall I urge the child of God to do this? No, I
will not so dishonour him ; surely he will believe
his own Father ! Surely, surely, it ought to be the
easiest thing in the world for the sons and daughters
of the Most High to believe in him who has given
them power to become the children of God ! My
brethren, let us not stagger at the promise through
unbelief, but believe up to the hilt !

Furthermore, *let us know the promises.* Should
we not carry them at our fingers' ends ? Should
we not know them better than anything else ? The
promises should be the classics of believers. If
you have not read the last new book, and have not
heard the last Act of the Government, yet know
right well what God the Lord hath said, and look
to see his word made good. We ought to be so
versed in Scripture as always to have at the tip of
our tongue the promise which most exactly meets
our case. We ought to be transcripts of Scripture:
the divine promise should be as much written upon
our hearts as upon the pages of the Book. It is a
sad pity that any child of God should be unaware
of the existence of the royal promise which would
enrich him. It is pitiful for any one of us to be
like the poor man, who had a fortune left him, of
which he knew nothing, and therefore he went on
sweeping a crossing, and begging for pence. What

is the use of having an anchor at home when your ship is in a storm at sea? What avails a promise which you cannot remember so as to plead it in prayer? Whatever else you do not know, do endeavour to be familiar with those words of the Lord which are more needful to our souls than bread to our bodies.

Let us also make use of the promises. A little while ago, a friend gave me a cheque for certain charities, and he said to me, "Be sure that you pay it into the bank to-day." You may rest assured that this was done. I do not keep cheques to look at, and play with: they go to the banker's, and the cash is received and expended.

The precious promises of our great God are expressly intended to be taken to him, and exchanged for the blessings which they guarantee. Prayer takes the promise to the Bank of Faith, and obtains the golden blessing. Mind how you pray. Make real business of it. Let it never be a dead formality. Some people pray a long time, but do not get what they are supposed to ask for, because they do not plead the promise in a truthful, business-like way. If you were to go into a bank, and stand an hour talking to the clerk, and then come out again without your cash, what would be the good of it? If I go to a bank, I pass my cheque across the counter, take up my money, and go about my business: that is the best way of praying. Ask for what you want, because the Lord has promised it. Believe that you have the blessing, and go forth to your work in full assurance of it. Go from your knees singing, because the promise is fulfilled: thus will your prayer be answered. It is not the length of your prayer, but the strength of your prayer which wins with God; and the strength of prayer lies in your faith in the promise which you have pleaded before the Lord.

Lastly, *talk about the promises*. Tell the King's household what the King has said. Never keep God's lamps under bushels. Promises are proclamations; exhibit them on the wall; read them aloud at the market-cross. Oh, that our conversation were more often sweetened with the precious promises of God! After dinner we often sit for half-an-hour, and pull our ministers to pieces, or scandalize our neighbours. How often is this the Sunday's amusement! It would be far better if we said, "Now, friend, quote a promise," and if the other replied, "And you mention a promise too." Then let each one speak according to his own personal knowledge concerning the Lord's fulfilment of those promises, and let every one present tell the story of the Lord's faithfulness to him. By such holy converse we should warm our own hearts, and gladden one another's spirits, and the Sabbath would thus be rightly spent.

Business men speak of their trade, travellers of their adventures, and farmers of their crops; should not we abundantly utter the memory of the Lord's goodness, and talk of his faithfulness? If we did so, we should all endorse Peter's statement, that our God has given unto us "*exceeding great and precious promises.*"

The Lord's Promise — the Rule of His Giving

"And the LORD gave Solomon wisdom, as he promised him."—
1 Kings v. 12.

HOW the Lord wrought wisdom in Solomon I do not know; but he promised that he would give him wisdom, and he kept his word. The more you think of this the more remarkable will the fact appear. Solomon was not born under the most hopeful circumstances for wisdom. As the darling child of a somewhat aged father, he was highly likely to be spoiled. As a young man who came to a throne before he was at all fitted for it in the course of nature, he was very likely to have made great blunders and mistakes. As a man of strong animal passions, which in the end overpowered him, he seemed more likely to prove a profligate than a philosopher. As a person possessing great wealth, unlimited power, and unvarying prosperity, he had little of that trying experience by which men acquire wisdom. Who were his teachers? Who taught him to be wise? His penitent mother may have set before him much of sound morality and religion, but she could never have imparted to him the eminent degree of wisdom which raised him above all other men and set him upon the pinnacle of renown. He knew more than others, and therefore could not have borrowed his wisdom from them. Sages sat at his feet, and his fame brought pilgrims from the ends of the earth: none could have been his tutors, since he surpassed them all. How did this man rise to absolute pre-eminence in wisdom, so as to make his name throughout all time the synonym for a wise man?

It is a very mysterious process this creation of a master mind. Who shall give a young man wisdom? You can impart knowledge to him, but not wisdom. No tutor, no master, no divine, can give another man wisdom: he has much ado to get a little of it for himself. Yet God gave Solomon largeness of heart as the sands of the sea, and wisdom unrivalled; for God can do all things. By operations known only to himself, the Lord produced in the young king a capacity for observation, reasoning, and prudent action, seldom if ever equalled. We have often admired the wisdom of Solomon; I invite you still more to admire the wisdom of Jehovah, by whom Solomon's marvellous genius was produced.

The reason why the Lord wrought this wonder upon Solomon was *because he had promised to do it, and he is sure to keep his word.* Many another text would serve my turn as well as this one, for all I desire to bring out of it is this—that whatever God has promised to anyone, he will surely give it to him. Whether it be wisdom to Solomon, or grace to my reader, if the Lord has made the promise, he will not allow it to be a dead letter. The God who performed his word in this very remarkable instance, where the matter was so entirely beyond human power, and was surrounded with such disadvantageous circumstances, will accomplish his promise in other cases, however difficult and mysterious the process of performance may be. God will always keep his word to the letter ; yea, and he will usually go beyond what the letter seems to mean. In this instance, while he gave Solomon wisdom, he also added to him riches, and a thousand other things which did not appear in the compact. "Seek ye first the kingdom of God and his righteousness, and all these things shall be added unto you." He who makes promises about infinite blessings, will throw in every-day things as if they were of small account, and were given in as a matter of course, like the grocer's paper and string with which he packs up our purchases.

From the case of Solomon, and thousands of a similar kind, we learn first that *the rule of God's giving is—as he has promised.*

The page of history sparkles with instances. The Lord promised to our fallen parents that the seed of the woman should bruise the serpent's head : behold, that wondrous Seed of the woman has appeared, and has gotten for himself, and for us, the glorious victory of our redemption ! In the fulfilment of that one promise we have security for the keeping of all the rest. When God promised to Noah that entering into the ark he would be safe, he found it so. Not one of those innumerable waves which destroyed the antediluvian world, could break into his place of safety. When God said to Abraham that he would give him a seed, and a land which should be the possession of that seed, it seemed impossible; but Abraham believed God, and in due time rejoiced to behold Isaac, and to see in him the promised heir. When the Lord promised to Jacob that he would be with him and do him good, he kept his word, and gave him the deliverance for which he wrestled at the brook Jabbok. That long-slumbering promise, that the seed of Israel should possess the land which flowed with milk and honey; it did seem as if it would never be accomplished, when the tribes were reduced to slavery in Egypt, and Pharaoh held them with iron grip, and would not let them go. But God, who undertook for his people, brought them out with a high hand, and with an outstretched arm, on the very day in which he promised to rescue them. He divided the Red Sea also, and he led his people through the wilderness, for he assured them that he would do so. He clave the Jordan in twain, and he drove out the Canaanites before his people, and gave to Israel the land for their inheritance, even as he had promised. The histories of the Lord's faithfulness are so many, that time would fail us to repeat them all. God's words have always in due time been justified by God's acts. God has dealt with men according to his promise. Whenever they have taken hold upon the promise, and said, "Do as thou hast said," God has responded to the plea, and proved that it is no vain thing to trust him. Throughout all time it has been God's unvarying rule to keep his word to the letter, and to the moment.

" This is big talk " says one ; then we will
descend to smaller talk. *It is God's way to keep
his promise to each individual.* We ourselves are
living witnesses that God forgets not his word.
Tens of thousands of us can testify that we have
trusted in him and have never been confounded. I
was once a broken-hearted sinner, cowering down
beneath the black cloud of almighty wrath, guilty
and self-condemned, and I felt that if I were
banished for ever from Jehovah's presence, I could
not say a word against the justice of the sentence.
When I read in his word, " If we confess our sins,
he is faithful and just to forgive us our sins," I
went to him. Tremblingly I resolved to test his
promise. I acknowledged my transgressions unto
the Lord, and he forgave the iniquity of my sin.
I am telling no idle tale, for the deep, restful peace
which came to my heart in the moment of forgive-
ness was such that it seemed as if I had begun
a new life ; as, indeed, I had.

This is how it came about : I heard, one Sabbath
day, a poor man speak upon that promise, " Look
unto me, and be ye saved, all ye ends of the earth."
I could not understand how a mere look to Christ
could save me. It seemed too simple an act to
effect so great a result ; but, as I was ready to try
anything, I LOOKED—*I looked to Jesus.*

It was all I did. It was all I could do. I looked
unto him who is set forth as a propitiation for
sin ; and in a moment I saw that I was reconciled
to God. I saw that if Jesus suffered in my stead,
I could not suffer too ; and that if he bore all my

sin, I had no more sin to bear. My iniquity must be blotted out if Jesus bore it in my stead, and suffered all its penalty. With that thought there came into my spirit a sweet sense of peace with God through Jesus Christ my Lord. The promise was true, and I found it to be so. It happened some six-and-thirty years ago, but I have never lost the sense of that complete salvation which I then found, nor have I lost that peace which so sweetly dawned upon my spirit. *Since then I have never relied in vain upon a promise of God. I have been placed in positions of great peril, have known great need, have felt sharp pain, and have been weighted with incessant anxieties; but the Lord has been true to every line of his word, and when I have trusted him he has carried me through everything without a failure. I am bound to speak well of him, and I do so.* TO THIS I SET MY HAND AND SEAL, *without hesitation or reserve.*

The experience of all believers is to much the same effect: we began our new lives of joy and peace by believing the promise-making God, and we continue to live in the same manner. A long list of fulfilled promises is present to our happy memories, awakening our gratitude and confirming our confidence. We have tested the faithfulness of our God year after year, in a great many ways, but always with the same result. We have gone to him with promises of the common things of life, relating to daily bread, and raiment, and children, and home; and the Lord has dealt graciously with us. We have resorted to him concerning sickness,

and slander, and doubt, and temptation ; and never
has he failed us.   In little things he has been
mindful of us : even the hairs of our head have been
numbered.   When it appeared very unlikely that
the promise could be kept, it has been fulfilled with
remarkable exactness.   We have been broken
down by the falseness of man, but we have exulted
and do exult in the truthfulness of God.   It brings
the tears into our eyes to think of the startling
ways in which Jehovah, our God, has wrought to
carry out his gracious promises.

> " Thus far we prove that promise good,
>   Which Jesus ratified with blood :
>   Still he is faithful, wise, and just,
>   And still in him believers trust."

Let me freely speak to all who trust in the Lord.
Children of God, has not your heavenly Father
been true to you ?   Is not this your constant experience, that you are always failing, but *he* never
fails ?   Well said our apostle, " Though we believe
not, he abideth faithful : he cannot deny himself."
We may interpret divine language in its broadest
sense, and we shall find that the Lord's promise is
kept to the utmost of its meaning.   The rule of his
giving is large and liberal : the promise is a great
vessel, and the Lord fills it to overflowing.   As the
Lord in Solomon's case gave him "*as he promised
him*," so will he in every instance so long as the
world standeth.   O reader ! believe the promise, and
thus prove yourself to be an inheritor of it.   May
the Holy Spirit lead you thus to do, for Jesus' sake !

The Rule without Exception

" Blessed be the LORD, that hath given rest unto his people Israel, according to all that he promised : there hath not failed one word of all his good promise, which he promised by the hand of Moses his servant."—I Kings viii. 56.

GOD *gives good things to men according to his promise.*

This is a matter of fact, and not a mere opinion. We declare it, and defy all the world to bring any evidence to disprove the statement.

Upon this point the writer is a personal witness. My experience has been long, and my observation has been wide; but I have never yet met with a person who trusted God, and found the Lord's promise fail him. I have seen many living men sustained under heavy trials by resting in the word of the Lord, and I have also seen many dying persons made triumphant in death by the same means; but I have never met with a believer who has been made ashamed of his hope because of his temporal afflictions, nor with one who on his deathbed has repented of trusting in the Lord. All my observation points the other way, and confirms me in the persuasion that the Lord is faithful to all who rely upon him. About this matter I should be prepared to make solemn affirmation in a court of justice. I would not utter a falsehood under the pretext of a pious fraud, but I would testify upon this important subject as an honest witness without reserve or equivocation. I never knew a man in the pangs of death lament that he trusted the Saviour. Nay, what is more, I have never heard that such a thing has happened anywhere at any time. If there had been such a case, the haters of the gospel would have advertised it high and low; every street would have heard the evil news; every preacher would have been confronted with it. We should have been met with pamphlets at the door of every church and chapel, reporting that such an one, who had lived a saintly life, and relied on the Redeemer's merits, had discovered in his last hours that he had been duped, and that the doctrine of the cross was all delusion. We challenge opponents to discover such an instance. Let them find it among rich or poor, old or young. Let the very fiend himself, if he can, bear witness to the failure of a single promise of the Living God. But it has not been said that Jehovah has deceived one of his people, and it never shall be said; for God is true to every word that he has ever spoken.

God never stoops to a lie. The mere supposition is blasphemous. Why should he be false? What is there about him that could cause him to break his word? It would be contrary to his nature. How could he be God and not be just and true? He cannot therefore violate his promise through any want of faithfulness.

Furthermore, the Omnipotent God never promises beyond his power. *We* frequently intend to act according to our word, but we find ourselves mastered by overwhelming circumstances, and our promise falls to the ground because we are unable to perform it. It can never be so with the Almighty God, for his ability is without limit. All things are possible with him.

Our promise may have been made in error, and we may afterwards discover that it would be wrong to do as we have said; but God is infallible, and therefore his word will never be withdrawn upon the ground of a mistake. Infinite wisdom has set its *imprimatur* upon every promise; each word of the Lord is registered by unerring judgment, and ratified by eternal truth.

Nor can the promise fail because of an alteration in the Divine Promiser. *We* change; poor, frail things that we are! But the Lord knows no variableness, neither shadow of a turning; hence his word abideth for ever the same. Because he changes not, his promises stand fast like the great mountains. "Hath he said, and shall he not do it?" Our strong consolation rests upon the immutable things of God.

Nor can the word of the Lord fall to the ground through forgetfulness on his part. With our tongues *we* outrun our hands; for, although we are willing, we fail in the performing because other things come in, and distract our attention. We forget, or we grow cold; but never is it so with the Faithful Promiser. His most ancient promise

is still fresh in his mind, and he means it now as
he did when he first uttered it. He is, in fact,
always giving the promise, since there is no time
with him. The old promises of Scripture are new
promises to faith ; for every word still proceedeth
out of the mouth of the Lord, to be bread for men.

*Because of all this, the word of the Lord deserves
all faith, both implicit and explicit.* We can trust
men too much, but we can never do so towards
God. It is the surest thing that has been, or that
can ever be. To believe his word is to believe what
none can fairly question. Has God said it ? Then
so it must be. Heaven and earth will pass away,
but God's word will never pass away. The laws of
nature may be suspended : fire may cease to burn,
and water to drown, for this would involve no un-
faithfulness in God ; but for his word to fail would
involve a dishonouring variableness in the character
and nature of the Godhead, and this can never
be. Let us set to our seal that God is true, and
never suffer a suspicion of his veracity to cross our
minds.

The immutable word of promise is, and ever
must be, the rule of God's giving. Consider a
little, while I make a further observation, namely,
that *against this no other rule can stand.* With
the rule of God's promise no other law, supposed
or real, can ever come into conflict.

The law of deserving is sometimes set up against
it, but it cannot prevail. "Oh," says one, "I cannot
think that God can or will save me, for there is
no good thing in me !" You speak rightly, and

your fear cannot be removed if God is to act towards you upon the rule of deserving. But if you believe on his Son Jesus, that rule will not operate, for the Lord will act towards you according to the rule of his promise. The promise was not founded upon your merits ; it was freely made, and it will be as freely kept. If you enquire how your ill-deservings can be met, let me remind you of Jesus who came to save you from your sins. The boundless deservings of the Lord Jesus are set to your account, and your terrible demerits are thereby neutralized once for all. The law of merit would sentence you to destruction as you stand in your own proper person; but he that believeth is not under law, but under grace; and under grace the great Lord deals with men according to pure mercy as revealed in his promise. Choose not to be self-righteous, or justice must condemn you ; be willing to accept salvation as a free gift bestowed through the exercise of the sovereign prerogative of God, who says, " I will have mercy on whom I will have mercy." Be humbly trustful in the grace of God which is revealed in Christ Jesus, and the promise shall be richly fulfilled to you.

Neither doth the Lord deal with men according to *the measure of their moral ability.* " Oh," says the seeker, " I think I might be saved if I could make myself better, or become more religious, or exercise greater faith ; but I am without strength. I cannot believe ; I cannot repent ; I cannot do anything aright !" Remember, then, that the Gracious God has not promised to bless you

according to the measure of your ability to serve
him, but according to the riches of his grace as
declared in his word. If his gifts were bestowed
according to your spiritual strength, you would get
nothing ; for you can do nothing without the Lord.
But as the promise is kept according to the infinity
of divine grace, there can be no question cast upon
it. You need not stagger at the promise through
unbelief, but reckon that he who has promised is
able also to perform. Do not limit the Holy One
of Israel by dreaming that his love is bounded by
your capacity. The volume of the river is not to
be computed by the dryness of the desert through
which it flows : there is no logical proportion
between the two. With half an eye one can see
that there is no calculating the extent of infinite love
by measuring human weakness. The operations of
almighty grace are not limited by mortal strength,
or want of strength. God's power will keep God's
promise. It is not your weakness that can defeat
God's promise, nor your strength that can fulfil the
promise : he that spoke the word will himself make
it good. It is neither your business nor mine to
keep God's promises : that is his office, and not
ours. Poor helpless one, attach your heavy waggon
of incapacity to the great engine of the promise,
and you will be drawn along the lines of duty
and blessing ! Though you are more dead than
alive, though you have more weakness than
strength, this shall not affect the certainty of the
divine engagement. The power of the promise lies
in him who made the promise. Look therefore

away from self to God. If you are faint, swoon away upon the bosom of the divine promise; if you count yourself dead, be buried in the grave where lie the bones of a promise, and you shall be made alive as soon as you touch them. What *we* can or cannot do is not the question; but everything hinges upon what the Lord can do. It is enough for us to keep our own contracts without attempting to keep God's promises. I should not like my fellow-man to doubt my solvency because a beggar who lives in the next street cannot pay his debts. Why, then, should I suspect the Lord because I have grave cause to distrust myself? *My* ability is quite another question from the faithfulness of God, and it is a pity to mix the two things. Let us not dishonour our God by dreaming that *his* arm has waxed short because our arm has grown weak or weary.

Neither must we measure God by the rule of our feelings. Often do we hear the lamentation—" I do not feel that I can be saved. I do not feel that such sin as mine can be forgiven. I do not feel it possible that my hard heart can ever be softened and renewed." This is poor, foolish talk. In what way can our feelings guide us in such matters? Do you feel that the dead in their graves can be raised again? Do you even feel that the cold of winter will be followed by the heat of summer? How can you feel these things? You believe them. To talk of feeling in the matter is absurd. Does the fainting man feel that he will revive? Is it not the nature of such a state to suggest death? Do dead

bodies feel that they will have a resurrection?
Feeling is out of the question.

God gave Solomon wisdom as he had promised
him, and he will give you what he has promised,
whatever your feelings may be. If you look through
the Book of Deuteronomy, you will see how often
Moses uses the expression *"as he promised."* He
says (Deut. i. 11), "The Lord bless you as he hath
promised you": he cannot pronounce on Israel a
larger benediction. That holy man viewed the
dealings of the Lord with constant admiration,
because they were "as he promised." In our case,
also, the rule of the Lord's dealings will be "as he
promised." Our experience of divine grace will
not be "as we now feel," but "as he promised."

While writing thus for the comfort of others, I
feel bound to confess that, personally, I am the
subject of very changeful feelings; but I have
learned to set very small store by them, either one
way or the other: above all, I have ceased to estimate the truth of the promise by my condition of
mind. To-day I feel so joyful that I could dance
to the tune of Miriam's timbrel; but perhaps when
I wake to-morrow morning I shall only be able
to sigh in harmony with Jeremiah's lamentations.
Has my salvation changed according to these
feelings? Then it must have had a very movable
foundation. Feelings are more fickle than the
winds, more unsubstantial than bubbles: are these
to be the gauge of the divine fidelity? States of
mind more or less depend upon the condition of
the liver or the stomach: are we to judge the

Lord by these? Certainly not. The state of the barometer may send our feelings up or down: can there be much dependence upon things so changeable? God does not suspend his eternal love upon our emotions that were to build a temple on a wave. We are saved according to facts, not according to fancies. Certain eternal verities prove us saved or lost; and those verities are not affected by our exhilarations or depressions. O my reader, do not set up your feelings as a test by which to try the truthfulness of the Lord! Such conduct is a sort of mingled insanity and wickedness. If the Lord has said the word, he will make it good, whether you feel triumphant or despondent.

Again, *God will not give to us according to the rule of probabilities.* It does seem very improbable that you, my friend, should be blessed of the Lord that made heaven and earth: but if you trust the Lord, you are favoured as surely as the Blessed Virgin herself, of whom it is said that all generations shall call her blessed; for it is written, " Blessed is she that believeth: for there shall be a performance of those things which were told her from the Lord." " O Lord of hosts, blessed is the man that trusteth in thee!" It may seem improbable that an old sinner, steeped in vice, should, by believing in Jesus, at once begin a new life; and yet it shall be so. It may seem very unlikely that a woman living in sin should hear that word, " He that believeth on him hath everlasting life," should immediately lay hold upon it, and at once receive everlasting life; yet it is true, for all that; and I have seen it so. Our God is a God of wonders. Things improbable, yea, impossible, with us, are every-day things with him. He causes the camel, despite its hump, to go through the needle's eye. He calleth the things which are not as though they were. Do you laugh at the very idea of your being saved? Let it not be the distrustful laugh of Sarai, but the joyous expectancy of Abraham. Believe on Jesus, and you shall laugh all over, inwardly and outwardly, not from incredulity, but for quite another reason. When we know God we do not cease to wonder, but we begin to be at home with wonders. Believe the promise of God's grace, and believing, you shall live in a new world which shall be always wonder-land to you. It is a happy thing to have such faith in God as to expect as certain that which to mere human judgment is most unlikely. "With God all things are possible": it is therefore possible that he should save every soul that believeth in Jesus. The law of gravitation acts in all cases, and so does the law of divine faithfulness: there are no exceptions to the rule that God will keep his covenant. Extreme cases, difficult cases, yea, impossible cases, are included within the circle of the Lord's word, and therefore none need despair, or even doubt. God's opportunity has come when man's extremity is reached. The worse the case, the more sure is it to be helped of the Lord. Oh, that my hopeless, helpless reader would do the Lord the honour to believe him, and leave all in his hands!

How long will it be ere men will trust their God? "O thou of little faith, wherefore didst thou doubt?" Oh, that we would settle it in our minds that we would never again distrust the Faithful One!

"Let God be true, but every man a liar." The Lord himself saith, "Is the LORD'S hand waxed short? Thou shalt see now whether my word shall come to pass unto thee or not" (Numbers xi. 23). Let not the Lord speak thus to us in anger, but let us believe and be sure that the solemn declarations of the Lord must be fulfilled. Speak no longer one to another, saying, "What is truth?" but know infallibly that the word of the Lord is sure, and endureth for ever.

Here is a promise for the reader to begin with : let him test it, and see if it be not true :—"CALL UPON ME IN THE DAY OF TROUBLE: I WILL DELIVER THEE, AND THOU SHALT GLORIFY ME" (Ps. l. 15).

Taking Possession of the Promise

"I am the LORD God of Abraham thy father, and the God of Isaac : the land whereon thou liest, to thee will I give it."

Genesis xxviii. 13.

TIMOROUS souls find much difficulty in laying hold upon the promises of God as being made to themselves : they fear that it would be presumption to grasp things so good and precious. As a general rule, we may consider that *if we have faith to grasp a promise, that promise is ours.* He who gives us the key which will fit the lock of his door intends that we should open the door and enter. There can never be presumption in humbly believing God ; there may be a great deal of it in daring to question his word. We are not likely to err in trusting the promise too far. Our failure lies in want of faith, not in excess of it. It would be hard to believe God too much : it is dreadfully common to believe him too little. "According to your faith be it unto you," is a benediction from which the Lord will never draw back. "If thou canst believe, all things are possible to him that believeth." It is written, "they could not enter in because of unbelief ;" but it is never said that one who entered in by faith was censured for his impertinence, and driven out again.

Jacob, according to the text with which we

have headed this chapter, took possession of the promised land by stretching himself upon it, and going to sleep. There is no surer way of taking possession of a promise than by placing your whole weight upon it, and then enjoying a hearty rest. " *The land whereon thou liest, to thee will I give it.*"

How often have I found the promise true to my own self when I have accepted it as truth, and acted upon it! I have stretched myself upon it as upon a couch, and left myself in the hands of the Lord ; and a sweet repose has crept over my spirit. Confidence in God realizes its own desires. The promise which our Lord made to those who seek favours in prayer runs thus,—" Believe that ye receive them, and ye shall have them." This sounds strange, but it is true ; it is according to the philosophy of faith. Say, by a realizing faith, "this promise is mine," and straightway it is yours. It is by faith that we " receive promises", and not by sight and sense.

The promises of God are not enclosures to be the private property of this saint or that, but they are an open common for all the dwellers in the parish of Holy Faith. No doubt there are persons who would, if they could, make a freehold of the stars, and a personal estate out of the sun and moon. The same greed might put a ring-fence around the promises ; but this cannot be done. As well might misers hedge in the song-birds, and claim the music of lark and thrush as their own sole inheritance, as propose to keep promises all to themselves. No, not the best of the saints can, even if they wished to do so, put a single word of the God of grace under lock and key. The promise is not only "unto you, and to your children," but also "to all that are afar off, even as many as the Lord our God shall call." What a comfort is this! Let us take up our common-rights, and possess by faith what the Lord has made ours by a covenant of salt.

Words spoken to Jacob belong equally to all believers. Hosea says of him, "Yea, he had power over the angel, and prevailed: he wept, and made supplication unto him: he found him in Bethel, *and there he spake with us.*" So that Jehovah spake with us when he spake with the patriarch. The wonders which God displayed at the Red Sea were wrought for all his people, for we read, "*there did we rejoice in him.*" (See Psalm lxvi. 6.) It is true we were not there, and yet the joy of Israel's victory is ours. The apostle quotes the word of the Lord to Joshua as if it were spoken to any and every child of God,—"He hath said, I will never leave *thee*, nor forsake *thee*" (Heb. xiii. 5), the fact being that no word of the Lord ends with the occasion which called it forth, or spends itself in blessing the individual to whom it was first addressed. All the promises are to believers who have faith enough to embrace them, and plead them at the throne of grace. What God is to one who trusts him, he will be to all such according to their circumstances and necessities.

The Bible has its eye upon each one of us as it utters its words of grace. A Bampton lecturer

has well said, "We, ourselves, and such as we are,
are the very persons whom Scripture speaks of;
and to whom, as men, in every variety of persuasive
form, it makes its condescending, though celestial,
appeal. The point worthy of observation is, to
note how a book of its description and its compass
should possess this versatility of power, this eye,
like that of a portrait uniformly fixed upon us, turn
where we will."

> "Eye of God's word! where'er we turn,
>   Ever upon us thy kind gaze
> Doth all our depths of woe discern,
>   Unravel every bosom's maze."
>
> "What word is this? whence know'st thou me?
>   All wondering cries the humbled heart,
> To hear thee that deep mystery,
>   The knowledge of itself, impart."

This singular personality of the word to each
one of a thousand generations of believers is one of
its greatest charms, and one of the surest proofs of
its divine inspiration. We treat our Bibles, not as
old almanacks, but as books for the present, new,
fresh, adapted for the hour. Abiding sweetness
dwells in undiminished freshness in the ancient
words upon which our fathers fed in their day.
Glory be to God, we are feasting on them still; or
if not, we ought to be; and can only blame ourselves if we do not!

The wells of Abraham served for Isaac, and
Jacob, and a thousand generations. Come, let us
let down our buckets, and with joy draw water out
of the old wells of salvation, digged in the far-off

days when our fathers trusted in the Lord, and he
delivered them! We need not fear that we shall
be superstitious or credulous. The promises of the
Lord are made to all who will believe them : faith
is itself a warrant for trusting. If thou *canst* trust,
thou mayest trust. After being fulfilled hundreds
of times, the words of promise still stand to be yet
further made good. Many a time and oft have we
stooped down to the spring-head in the meadow,
and quaffed a cooling draught ; it is just as full
and free, and we may drink to-day with as much
confidence as if we now stooped for the first time.
Men do not keep their promises over and over
again : it would be unreasonable to expect it of
them. They are cisterns, but thou, O Lord, art a
fountain! All my fresh springs are in thee.

Come, reader, imitate Jacob! As he laid him
down in a certain place, and took of the stones of
the place for his pillows, so do thou. Here is the
whole Bible for a couch, and here are certain
promises to serve as pillows ; lay down thy burdens,
and thyself also, and take thy rest. Behold, this
Scripture and its promises are henceforth thine,—
" *the land whereon thou liest, to thee will I give it.*"

Endorsing the Promise

"I believe God, that it shall be even as it was told me."

Acts xxvii. 25.

PAUL had received a special promise, and he openly avowed his faith in it. He believed that God would fulfil every detail of that promise. In this way he set to his seal that God is true. We are each one of us bound to do this with those words of the Lord which are suitable to our case. This is what I mean by the head-line—*endorsing the promise.*

A friend gives me for the Orphanage a cheque, which runs thus, "Pay to the order of C. H. Spurgeon, the sum of £10." His name is good, and his bank is good, but I get nothing from his kindness till I put my own name at the back of his cheque or draft. It is a very simple act: I merely sign my name, and the banker pays me: but the signature cannot be dispensed with.

There are many nobler names than mine, but none of these can be used instead of my own. If I wrote the Queen's name, it would not avail me. If the Chancellor of the Exchequer placed his signature on the back of the document, it would be in vain. I must myself affix my own name. Even so each one must personally accept, adopt, and endorse the promise of God by his own individual faith, or he will derive no benefit from it.

If you were to write Miltonic lines in honour of the bank, or exceed Tennyson in verses in praise of the generous benefactor of the orphans, it would avail nothing. The choicest language of men and of angels would count for nothing; what is absolutely requisite is the personal signature of the party who is named as the receiver. However fine might be the sketch which an artistic pencil might draw upon the back of the draft, that also would be of no sort of service: the simple, self-written name is demanded, and nothing will be accepted instead of it. We must believe the promise, each one for himself, and declare that we know it to be true, or it will bring us no blessing. No good works, or ceremonial performances, or rapturous feelings, can supply the place of a simple confidence. " He that cometh to God *must* believe that he is, and that he is a rewarder of them that diligently seek him." Some things may be or may not be, but this *must* be.

The promise may be said to run thus, " I promise to pay to the order of any sinner who will believe on me the blessing of eternal life." The sinner *must* write his name on the back of the draft; but nothing else is asked of him. He believes the promise, he goes to the throne of grace with it, and he looks to receive the mercy which it guaranteed to him. He shall have that mercy: he cannot fail to do so. It is written, " He that believeth on the Son hath everlasting life "; and so it is.

Paul believed that all in the ship with him would escape *because God had promised it.* He accepted the promise as ample security for the fact, and acted accordingly. He was calm amid the storm ; he gave his comrades sage and sensible advice as to breaking their fast ; and, in general, he managed matters as a man would do who was sure of a happy escape from the tempest. Thus he treated God as he should be treated, namely, with unquestioning confidence. An upright man likes to be trusted; it would grieve him if he saw that he was regarded with suspicion. Our faithful God is jealous of his honour, and cannot endure that men should treat him as if he could be false. Unbelief provokes the Lord above any other sin : it touches the apple of his eye, and cuts him to the quick. Far be it from us to perpetrate so infamous a wrong towards our heavenly Father ; let us believe him up to the hilt, placing no bounds to our hearty reliance upon his word.

Paul openly avowed his confidence in the promise. It is well that we should do the same. Just at this time, bold, outspoken testimonies to the truth of God are greatly needed, and may prove to be of seven-fold value. The air is full of doubt ; indeed, few really and substantially believe. Such a man as George Müller, who believes in God for the maintenance of two thousand children, is a rare personage. " When the Son of man cometh, shall he find faith on the earth ? " Therefore let us speak out. Infidelity has defied us ; let no man's heart fail him, but let us meet the giant with the sling and stone of actual experience, and unflinching witness. *God does keep his promise, and we know it.* We dare endorse every one of his promises. Ay, we would do it with our blood if it were needful! The word of the Lord endureth for ever, and of this we are undaunted witnesses, even all of us who are called by his name.

The Promise Used for This Life

"Godliness is profitable unto all things, having promise of the life that now is, and of that which is to come."—1 Tim. iv. 8.

A SORT of affectation prevents some Christians from treating religion as if its sphere lay among the common places of daily life. It is to them transcendental and dreamy; rather a creation of pious fiction than a matter of fact. They believe in God, after a fashion, for things spiritual, and for the life which is to be; but they totally forget that true godliness hath the promise of the life which now is, as well as of that which is to come. To them it would seem almost a profanation to pray about the small matters of which daily life is made up. Perhaps they will be startled if I venture to suggest that this should make them question the reality of their faith. If it cannot bring them help in little troubles of life, will it support them in the greater trials of death? If it cannot profit them as to food and raiment, what can it do for them as to the immortal spirit?

In the life of Abraham we perceive that his faith had to do with all the events of his earthly pilgrimage; it was connected with his removals from one country to another, with the separation of a nephew

from his camp, with fighting against invaders, and
specially with the birth of the long-promised son.
No part of the patriarch's life was outside the circle
of his faith in God.   Towards the close of his life it
is said, "and the Lord had blessed Abraham in
all things," which includes temporals as well as
spirituals.   In Jacob's case the Lord promised him
bread to eat, and raiment to put on, and the bring-
ing of him to his father's house in peace ; and all
these things are of a temporal and earthly character.
Assuredly these first believers did not spirit away
the present blessings of the covenant, or regard it
as an airy, mystical matter to believe in God.   One
is struck with the want of any line of demarcation
between secular and sacred in their lives ; they
journeyed as pilgrims, fought like Crusaders, ate
and drank like saints, lived as priests, and spake as
prophets.   Their life was their religion, and their
religion was their life.   They trusted God, not
merely about certain things of higher import, but
about everything, and hence, even a servant from
one of their houses, when he was sent on an errand,
prayed, "O Lord God of my master, prosper the
way which I go !"   This was genuine faith, and it
is ours to imitate it, and no longer to allow the
substance of the promise, and the life of faith, to
evaporate in mere sentimental and visionary fancies.
If trust in God is good for anything, it is good for
everything within the line of the promise, and it is
certain that the life which now is lies within that
region.

Let my reader observe and practically use such

words of God as these,—" Ye shall serve the Lord
your God, and he shall bless thy bread, and thy
water ; and I will take sickness away from the
midst of thee " (Ex. xxiii. 25). "Trust in the Lord,
and do good ; so shalt thou dwell in the land, and
verily thou shalt be fed " (Ps. xxxvii. 3). "Surely
he shall deliver thee from the snare of the fowler,
and from the noisome pestilence. He shall cover
thee with his feathers, and under his wings shalt
thou trust : his truth shall be thy shield and buckler.
Thou shalt not be afraid for the terror by night ;
nor for the arrow that flieth by day ; nor for the
pestilence that walketh in darkness ; nor for the
destruction that wasteth at noonday. A thousand
shall fall at thy side, and ten thousand at thy right
hand ; but it shall not come nigh thee " (Ps. xci.
3—7). "He shall deliver thee in six troubles :
yea, in seven there shall no evil touch thee "
(Job v. 19). "He that walketh righteously, and
speaketh uprightly ; he that despiseth the gain of
oppressions, that shaketh his hands from holding of
bribes, that stoppeth his ears from hearing of blood,
and shutteth his eyes from seeing evil ; he shall
dwell on high : his place of defence shall be the
munitions of rocks : bread shall be given him ; his
waters shall be sure " (Is. xxxiii. 15, 16). "For the
Lord God is a sun and shield : the Lord will give
grace and glory : no good thing will he withhold
from them that walk uprightly " (Ps. lxxxiv. 11).
"No weapon that is formed against thee shall
prosper ; and every tongue that shall rise against
thee in judgment thou shalt condemn. This is the

heritage of the servants of the Lord, and their righteousness is of me, saith the Lord " (Is. liv. 17).

Our Saviour intended faith to be our *quietus* concerning daily cares, or he would not have said, " Therefore I say unto you, take no thought for your life, what ye shall eat, or what ye shall drink ; nor yet for your body, what ye shall put on. Is not the life more than meat, and the body than raiment ? Behold the fowls of the air : for they sow not, neither do they reap, nor gather into barns ; yet your heavenly Father feedeth them. Are ye not much better than they ? " (Matt. vi. 25, 26.)   What else but the exercise of faith concerning temporal things could he have meant when he used the following language ?—" And seek not ye what ye shall eat, or what ye shall drink, neither be ye of doubtful mind.   For all these things do the nations of the world seek after : and your Father knoweth that ye have need of these things " (Luke xii. 29, 30).

Paul meant the same when he wrote, " Be careful for nothing ; but in every thing by prayer and supplication with thanksgiving let your requests be made known unto God.   And the peace of God, which passeth all understanding, shall keep your hearts and minds through Christ Jesus " (Phil. iv. 6, 7).

He who is gone to prepare heaven for us will not leave us without provision for the journey thither. God does not give us heaven as the Pope gave England to the Spanish King—*if he could get it :* but he makes the road sure, as well as the end.

Now, our earthly necessities are as real as our spiritual ones, and we may rest sure that the Lord will supply them. He will send us those supplies in the way of promise, prayer, and faith, and so make them a means of education for us. He will fit us for Canaan by the experience of the wilderness.

To suppose that temporal things are too little for our condescending God, is to forget that he observes the flight of sparrows, and counts the hairs of his people's heads. Besides, everything is so little to him, that, if he does not care for the little, he cares for nothing. Who is to divide affairs by size or weight? The turning-point of history may be a minute circumstance. Blessed is the man to whom nothing is too small for God; for certainly nothing is too small to cause us sorrow, or to involve us in peril. A man of God once lost a key: he prayed about it, and found it. It was reported of him as a strange circumstance. Indeed, it was nothing unusual: some of us pray about everything, and tremble lest the infinitesimal things should not be sanctified by the word of God and prayer. It is not the including of trifles which is any trouble to our consciences, but the omission of them. We are assured that, when our Lord gave his angels charge to guard our feet from stones in the way, he placed all the details of our life under heavenly care, and we are glad to commit all things to his keeping.

It is one of the abiding miracles of the present dispensation that in Christ we have continual peace under all trials, and through him we have power in prayer to obtain from the Lord all things necessary for this life and godliness. It has been the writer's lot to test the Lord hundreds of times about temporal needs, being driven thereto by the care of orphans and students. Prayer has many, many times brought opportune supplies, and cleared away serious difficulties. I know that faith can fill a purse, provide a meal, change a hard heart, procure a site for a building, heal sickness, quiet insubordination, and stay an epidemic. Like money in the worldling's hand, faith in the hand of the man of God "answereth all things." All things in heaven, and earth, and under the earth, answer to the command of prayer. Faith is not to be imitated by a quack, nor simulated by a hypocrite; but where it is real, and can grasp a divine promise with firm grip, it is a great wonder-worker. How I wish that my reader would so believe in God as to lean upon him in all the concerns of his life! This would lead him into a new world, and bring to him such confirmatory evidence as to the truth of our holy faith that he would laugh sceptics to scorn. Child-like faith in God provides sincere hearts with a practical prudence, which I am inclined to call— sanctified common-sense. The simple-minded believer, though laughed at as an idiot, has a wisdom about him which cometh from above, and effectually baffles the cunning of the wicked. Nothing puzzles a malicious enemy like the straightforward unguardedness of an out-and-out believer.

He that believes his God is not afraid of evil

tidings, for his heart has found a calm fixity in trusting in the Lord.   In a thousand ways this faith sweetens, enlarges, and enriches life.   Try it, dear reader, and see if it does not yield you an immeasurable wealth of blessedness !   It will not save you from trouble, for the promise is, "These things I have spoken unto you, that in me ye might have peace.   In the world ye shall have tribulation : but be of good cheer; I have overcome the world " (John xvi. 33) : but it will cause you to glory in tribulations also, "knowing that tribulation worketh patience; and patience, experience ; and experience, hope : and hope maketh not ashamed ; because the love of God is shed abroad in our hearts by the Holy Ghost which is given unto us " (Rom. v. 3-5).

My faith not only flies to heaven,
But walks with God below ;
To me are all things daily given,
While passing to and fro.

The promise speaks of worlds above,
But not of these alone ;
It feeds and clothes me *now* with love,
And makes this world my own.

I trust the Lord, and he replies,
In things both great and small.
He honours faith with prompt supplies ;
Faith honours *him* in all.

Searching Out the Promise

"Thou hast promised this goodness unto thy servant."—
2 Samuel vii. 28.

KING David knew what the Lord had engaged to give him, and he referred to it specially in his prayer as "this good thing." *(Revised Version.)* We greatly need to be more definite in our supplications than we usually are : we pray for everything in such a way that we practically pray for nothing. It is well to know what we want. Hence our Lord said to the blind man, "What wilt thou that I should do unto thee ?" He wished him to be aware of his own needs, and to be filled with earnest desires concerning those needs : these are valuable ingredients in the composition of prayer.

Knowing what we need, the next business is to find that the Lord has promised us this particular blessing, for then we can go to God with the utmost confidence, and look for the fulfilment of his word. To this end we should diligently search the Scriptures, looking much to the cases of other believers which are like our own, and endeavouring to light upon that particular utterance of divine grace which is suitable to ourselves in our present circumstances. The more exact the agreement of the promise to the case, the greater

the comfort which it will yield. In this school the
believer will learn the value of plenary, ay, of
verbal inspiration; for in his own instance he may
have to dwell upon so slight a matter as the
number of a noun, as Paul did when quoting the
promise made to Abraham he remarks, " Now to
Abraham and his *seed* were the promises made.
He saith not, And to *seeds*, as of many; but as of
one, And to thy *seed*, which is Christ" (Gal. iii. 16).

We may rest assured that somewhere in the
inspired page there is a promise fitting the occasion.
The infinite wisdom of God is seen in his having
given us a revelation which meets the innumerable
varieties of his people's conditions. Not a single
trial is overlooked, however peculiar it may be.
As there is food specially adapted for every living
thing upon the face of the earth, so there is suitable
support for every child of God in the volume of
inspiration. If we do not find a fitting promise, it
is because we do not look for it; or having found
it, have not yet perceived its full meaning.

A homely comparison may be useful here. You
have lost the key of a chest, and after trying all
the keys you possess, you are obliged to send out
for a smith. The tradesman comes with a huge
bunch of keys of all sorts and sizes. To you they
appear to be a singular collection of rusty instru-
ments. He looks at the lock, and then he tries first
one key and then another. He has not touched it
yet; and your treasures are still out of your reach.
Look, he has found a likely key: it almost touches
the bolt, but not quite. He is evidently on the

right track now. At last the chest is opened, for
the right key has been found. This is a correct
representation of many a perplexity. You cannot
get at the difficulty so as to deal with it aright, and
find your way to a happy result. You pray, but
have not the liberty in prayer which you desire. A
definite promise is what you want. You try one
and another of the inspired words, but they do not
fit. The troubled heart sees reasons to suspect
that they are not strictly applicable to the case in
hand, and so they are left in the old Book for use
another day; for they are not available in the
present emergency. You try again, and in due
season a promise presents itself, which seems to
have been made for the occasion; it fits as exactly
as a well-made key fits the wards of the lock for
which it was originally prepared. Having found
the identical word of the living God, you hasten to
plead it at the throne of grace, saying, "O my
Lord, thou hast promised this good thing unto
thy servant; be pleased to grant it!" The matter
is ended; sorrow is turned to joy; prayer is heard.

Frequently the Holy Spirit brings to our remembrance with life and power words of the Lord which
else we might have forgotten. He also sheds a new
light upon well-remembered passages, and so reveals
a fulness in them which we had little suspected.
In cases known to me, the texts have been singular,
and for a while the person upon whose mind they
were impressed could hardly see their bearing.
For years one heart was comforted with the words
"His soul shall dwell at ease; and his seed shall

inherit the earth." This passage was seldom out
of his mind ; indeed, it seemed to him to be per-
petually whispered in his ear. The special relation
of the promise to his experience was made known by
the event. A child of God, who mourned his years
of barrenness, was lifted at once into joy and peace
by that seldom-quoted word, "I will restore to you
the years that the locust hath eaten." The bitter
experiences of David as to slander and malice led
to the utterance of consoling promises, which have
been a thousand times appropriated by obscure and
broken-hearted Christians when afflicted with "trials
of cruel mockings." Before this dispensation shall
close, we doubt not that every sentence of Scripture
will have been illustrated by the life of one or other
of the saints. Perhaps some obscure and little-
understood promise is still lying by until he shall
come for whom it was specially written. If we
may so say, there is one rusty key on the bunch
which has not yet found its lock ; but it will find
it before the history of the church is finished : we
may be sure of that.

*The word of the Lord which would remove our
present discomfort may be close at hand, and yet
we may not be aware of it.* With singular knowledge of human experience, John Bunyan represents
the prisoner of Doubting Castle as finding in his
own bosom the key called Promise, which opened
every door in that gloomy prison-house. We often
lie in durance vile when the means of obtaining
fullest liberty proffers itself to us. If we would
but open our eyes, we should, like Hagar, see a

well of water close at hand, and wonder why we
thought of dying of thirst.   At this moment, O
tempted brother, there is a word of the Lord
awaiting thee!   As the manna fell early in the
morning, and lay ready for the Israelites to gather
it as soon as ever they left their beds, so does the
promise of the Lord wait for thy coming.   The
oxen and the fatlings of grace are killed, and all
things are ready for thine immediate comfort.   The
mountain is full of chariots of fire, and horses of
fire, prepared for thy deliverance ; the prophet of
the Lord can see them, and if thine eyes were
opened thou wouldst see them too.   Like the
lepers at the gate of Samaria, it would be foolish
for thee to sit where thou art, and die.   Bestir
thyself, for close at hand lavish mercy is poured
forth, exceeding abundantly above all that thou
dost ask, or even think.   Only believe, and enter
into rest.

For the poor, the sick, the faint, the erring, there
are words of good cheer which they alone can enjoy.
For the fallen, the desponding, the despairing, the
dying, there are cordials which are compounded
with an eye to their peculiar maladies.   The widow
and the fatherless have their promises, and so have
captives, travellers, shipwrecked mariners, aged
persons, and those in the article of death.   No one
ever wanders where a promise does not follow him.
An atmosphere of promise surrounds believers as
the air surrounds the globe.   I might almost call it
omnipresent, and say of it, "Thou hast beset me
behind and before, and laid thine hand upon me.

Such knowledge is too wonderful for me; it is high, I cannot attain unto it. Whither shall I go from thy spirit? Or whither shall I flee from thy presence?" (Psalm cxxxix. 5, 6, 7.) No depth of darkness can hide us from the covenant of promise; say, rather, in its presence the night shineth as the day. Wherefore, let us take courage, and by faith and patience wait in the land of our exile till the day of our home-bringing. So shall we, like the rest of the heirs of salvation, "inherit the promise."

Certain covenant engagements, made with the Lord Jesus Christ, as to his elect and redeemed ones, are altogether without condition so far as we are concerned; but many other wealthy words of the Lord contain stipulations which must be carefully regarded, or we shall not obtain the blessing. One part of my reader's diligent search must be directed towards this most important point. God will keep his promise to thee; only see thou to it that the way in which he conditions his engagement is carefully observed of thee. Only when we fulfil the requirement of a conditional promise can we expect that promise to be fulfilled to us. He hath said, "He that believeth in Jesus shall be saved." If thou believest in the Lord Jesus Christ, it is certain that thou shalt be saved; but not else. In the same way, if the promise is made to prayer, to holiness, to reading the word, to abiding in Christ, or whatever else it may be, give thy heart and soul to the thing commanded, that the blessing may become thine. In some cases, great blessedness is not realized because known duties are neglected

The promise cannot enter because "sin lieth at the door." Even an unknown duty may whip us with "a few stripes," and a few strokes may greatly mar our happiness. Let us endeavour to know the Lord's will in all things, and then let us obey it without a trace of hesitation. It is not of the way of our wilfulness, but of the tracks of divine wisdom that we read, "Her ways are ways of pleasantness, and all her paths are peace."

Do not undervalue the grace of the promise because it has a condition appended to it ; for, as a rule, it is in this way made doubly valuable,—the condition being in itself another blessing, which the Lord has purposely made inseparable from that which thou desirest, that thou mayest gain two mercies while seeking only one. Moreover, remember that the condition is grievous to those only who are not heirs of the promise : to them it is as a thorn hedge, keeping them off from the comfort to which they have no right ; but to thee it is not grievous, but pleasant, and it is therefore no hindrance to thine access to the blessing. Those requirements, which show a black cloud and darkness to the Egyptians, have a bright side for the Israelites, and give light by night to them. To us the Lord's yoke is easy, and in taking it upon us we find rest unto our souls. See then that thou note the wording of the promise, and carry out all its precepts, that all good things may come to thee.

If thou art a believer in the Lord Jesus, all the promises are thine ; and among them is one for this very day of the month, and for this particular place wherein thou art now encamped: wherefore search the roll of thy Magna Charta, and find out thy portion for this hour. Of all the promises which the Lord hath given in his Book, he hath said, "No one of these shall fail, none shall want its mate, for my mouth hath commanded them." Therefore trust, and be not afraid. Whatever else may prove a failure, the promise of God never will. Treasure laid up in this Bank is beyond all hazard. "It is better to trust in the Lord than to put confidence in princes." Let us sing at every remembrance of the God of truth and grace.

> " Tell of his wondrous faithfulness,
>   And sound his power abroad ;
>   Sing the sweet promise of his grace,
>   And the performing God.
>
>   He that can dash whole worlds to death,
>   And make them when he please ;
>   He speaks, and that almighty breath
>   Fulfils his great decrees.
>
>   His very word of grace is strong
>   As that which built the skies ;
>   The voice that rolls the stars along
>   Speaks all the promises."

The Time of the Promise

"The time of the promise drew nigh."—Acts vii. 17.

THOMAS BROOKS reminds us that the mercies of God are not styled the *swift*, but "the *sure* mercies of David." There is nothing of hurry about the procedure of the Lord : it may even seem that the chariots of his grace are long in coming. It is by no means an unusual circumstance for the saints to be heard crying, " O Lord, how long ? " It is written "the glory of the Lord shall be thy rereward " (Is. lviii. 8). Now the guard of the rear comes up last, but it does come. God may some-times make us wait ; but we shall see in the end that he is as surely the Omega as the Alpha of his people's salvation. Let us never distrust him, but though the vision tarry, let us wait for it ; because it will surely come, it will not tarry (Hab. ii. 3).

There once sailed from the port of London a vessel, which the owner called the *Swift-sure*, because he hoped it would prove both safe and speedy. Truly this is a fit name for the Lord's mercy : it is both swift and sure. David may not have said so in the text which Brooks quotes, but he often said as much and even more in others. Did he not say " He rode upon a cherub, and did fly : yea, he did fly upon the wings of the wind " ?

The Lord is not slow to hear the cries of his people. He has a set time to favour Zion, and when that set time is come there will be no delay.

The date for its fulfilment is an important part of a promise ; indeed, it enters into the essence of it. It would be unjust to delay the payment of a debt ; and the obligation to keep one's word is of the same nature. The Lord is prompt to the moment in carrying out his gracious engagements. The Lord had threatened to destroy the world with a flood, but he waited the full time of respite until Noah had entered the ark ; and then, on the selfsame day, the fountains of the great deep were broken up. He had declared that Israel should come out of Egypt, and it was so : "And it came to pass at the end of the four hundred and thirty years, even the selfsame day it came to pass, that all the hosts of the Lord went out from the land of Egypt" (Exodus xii. 41). According to Daniel, the Lord numbers the years of his promise, and counts the weeks of his waiting. As for the greatest promise of all, namely, the sending of his Son from heaven, the Lord was not behind-hand in that great gift, "but when the fulness of the time was come, God sent forth his Son, made of a woman." Beyond all question, the Lord our God keeps his word to the moment.

When we are in need, we may be urgent with the Lord to come quickly to our rescue, even as David pleaded in the seventieth Psalm,—"Make haste, O God, to deliver me ; make haste to help me, O Lord." (Verse 1.)   "I am poor and needy :

make haste unto me, O God: thou art my help and my deliverer ; O Lord, make no tarrying." (Verse 5.) The Lord even condescends to describe himself as making speed to carry out his gracious engagements, saying, "I the Lord will hasten it in his time" (Isaiah lx. 22). But we must not pray in this fashion as though we had the slightest fear that the Lord could or would be dilatory, or that he needed us to quicken his diligence. No. "The Lord is not slack concerning his promise, as some men count slackness" (2 Peter iii. 9). Our God is slow to anger, but in deeds of grace "his word runneth very swiftly" (Psalm cxlvii. 15). Sometimes his speed to bless his people outstrips time and thought : as, for instance, when he fulfils that ancient declaration, "It shall come to pass, that before they call, I will answer ; and while they are yet speaking, I will hear " (Isaiah lxv. 24).

Yet there are delays in the answers to our prayers. As the husbandman does not reap to-day that which he sowed yesterday, so neither do we always at once obtain from the Lord that which we seek of him. The door of grace does open, but not to our first knocks. Why is this? It is because the mercy will be all the greater for being longer on the road. There is a time for every purpose under heaven, and everything is best in its time. Fruit ripens in its season ; and the more seasonable it is the better it is. Untimely mercies would be only half mercies; therefore the Lord withholds them till they have come to their perfection. Even heaven itself will be all the better because it will not be ours till it is prepared for us, and we are prepared for it.

Love presides over the arrangements of grace, and strikes upon the bell when the best moment has arrived. God blesses us by his temporary delays, as well as by his prompt replies. We are not to doubt the Lord because his time has not yet come : that would be to act like petulant children, who must have a thing at the instant, or else they think they shall never have it. A waiting God is the true object of confidence to his waiting people. "Therefore will the Lord wait, that he may be gracious unto you" (Is. xxx. 18). His compassions fail not even when his gracious operations appear to be suspended, and our griefs are deepened. Yea, it is because he loves us so much that he tries us by delaying his answers of peace. It is with our Father in heaven even as it was with our Lord on earth: "Now Jesus loved Martha, and her sister, and Lazarus. When he had heard therefore that he was sick, he abode two days still in the same place where he was" (John xi. 5, 6). Love closes the hand of divine bounty, and restrains the outflow of favour, when it sees that a solid gain will ensue from a period of trial.

Perhaps the time of the promise has not yet come, because our trial has not yet fulfilled its design. The chastening must answer its purpose, or it cannot be brought to an end. Who would desire to see the gold taken out of the fire before its dross is consumed ? Wait, O precious thing, till thou hast gained the utmost of purity! These furnace moments are profitable. It would be unwise to shorten such golden hours. The time of the promise corresponds with the time most enriching to heart and soul.

Perhaps, moreover, we have not yet displayed sufficient submission to the divine will. Patience has not yet had her perfect work. The weaning process is not accomplished : we are still hankering after the comforts which the Lord intends us for ever to outgrow. Abraham made a great feast when his son Isaac was weaned ; and, peradventure, our heavenly Father will do the same with us. Lie down, proud heart! Quit thine idols ; forsake thy fond dotings ; and the promised peace will come unto thee.

Possibly, also, we have not yet performed a duty which will become the turning-point of our condition. The Lord turned again the captivity of Job when he prayed for his friends. It may be that the Lord will make us useful to a relative or other friend before he will favour us with personal consolations : we are not to see the face of our Joseph except our brother be with us. Some ordinance of the Lord's house may lie neglected, or some holy work may be left undone ; and this may hinder the promise. Is it so ? "Are the consolations of God small with thee? Is there any secret thing with thee?" Peradventure we are yet to vow unto the Lord, and make a notable sacrifice unto him, and then will he bring his covenant to mind. Let him not have to complain, "Thou hast bought me no sweet cane with money." Rather let us accept his challenge, " Bring ye all the tithes into the store-house, and prove me now herewith, saith the Lord of hosts, if I will not open you the windows of heaven, and pour you out a blessing" (Mal. iii. 10).

God's promises are so dated as to secure his glory in their fulfilment, and this must be enough for us when we can see no other reason for delay. It may be necessary for us to be made more fully aware of our need, and the great value of the blessings which we crave. That which too lightly comes may be too lightly prized. Perhaps our ungrateful spirits need tutoring to thankfulness by an education of waiting. We might not loudly sing if we did not deeply sigh. Wanting and waiting lead to panting and pleading; and these in due time lead to joying and rejoicing.

If all things could be known to us as they are known to God, we should bless him with all our hearts for keeping us under the smarting rod, and not sparing us for our crying. If we could know the end as well as the beginning, we should praise the Lord for closed doors, and frowning looks, and unanswered petitions. Surely, if we knew that the Lord's great purposes were answered by our continuing without the pleasures we desire, and bearing the evils which we dread, we should cry aloud to be left in our poverty, and to be shut up in our pain. If we can glorify God by being denied what we seek, we desire to be denied. Greatest of all our prayers, and sum of all the rest, is this one, "*Nevertheless, not as I will, but as thou wilt.*"

The Promises in Possession
through the Spirit

"That holy Spirit of promise, which is the earnest of our inheritance until the redemption of the purchased possession, unto the praise of his glory."—Eph. i. 13, 14.

I N a very true and real sense the things promised in the covenant are already the property of believers. "All things *are* yours." The great Father might truly say to each one of the sons who abide in his house, "All that I have is thine." The inheritance is already ours, say the old divines, *in promisso, in pretio, in principiis;* that is to say, in the promise of God, in the price paid by the Lord Jesus, and in its first principles which are infused into us by the Holy Spirit. In his sure promise the Father has already "blessed us with all spiritual blessings in heavenly places in Christ": he has not only resolved to enrich us in the future, but even now he has endowed us with the treasures of his love. The Lord Jesus has not merely made us heirs of an infinite estate in the ages to come, but he has brought us into immediate enjoyment of a present portion; as saith the Scripture, "In whom also we have obtained an inheritance."

The Holy Spirit is in many ways the means of making the promised heritage ours even now. *By*

him we are " sealed."   We know of a surety that
the inheritance is ours, and that we ourselves belong
to the great Heir of all things.   The operations of
the Holy Ghost upon us in our regeneration, and
his abiding in us by sanctification, are certificates
of our being in grace, and of our being inheritors of
glory.   Beyond all other testimonies of our being
saved, there stands this sure and certain evidence,
namely, that the Spirit of the living God rests upon
us.   Repentance, faith, spiritual life, holy desires,
upward breathings, and even "groanings which cannot be uttered," are all proofs that the Holy Ghost
is working upon us; and working in a way peculiar
to the heirs of salvation.   Life breathed into us by
the Holy Ghost is the great seal of the kingdom of
God to our souls.   We need no dreams, nor visions,
nor mystic voices, nor rapturous feelings: the
quickening and renewing of the Holy Ghost are
better seals than these.   The Spirit of promise
does not prepare men for a blessedness which shall
never be theirs.   He who hath wrought us to the
self-same thing will secure that blessing to us for
which he hath prepared us.   The faintest impress
of the seal of the Spirit is a better attestation of
our part and lot with the people of God than all
the presumptuous inferences which self-conceit can
draw from its heated fancies.

Nor is the Holy Spirit only the seal of the
inheritance, *he is also the earnest of it.*   Now an
earnest is a part of the thing itself, given as a
guarantee that the remainder will be forthcoming
in due season.   If a man is paid a part of his six-

days' wage in the middle of the week, it is earnest-money. In this an earnest differs from a pledge, for a pledge is returned when we receive that which it secured ; but an earnest is not returned, for it is a part of that which is promised. Even so the Holy Spirit is himself a great portion of the inheritance of the saints ; and in having him we have the beginning of perfectness, of heaven, of eternal glory. He is everlasting life, and his gifts, graces, and workings are the first principles of endless felicity. In having the Holy Ghost we have the kingdom which it is our Father's good pleasure to give to his chosen.

This will be made clear by a few moments' reflection. Heaven will much consist in holiness ; and it is clear that, as far as the Holy Ghost makes us holy here, he has implanted the beginnings of heaven. Heaven is victory ; and each time that we overcome sin, Satan, the world, and the flesh, we have foretastes of the unfading triumph which causes the waving of palms in the New Jerusalem. Heaven is an endless Sabbath ; and how can we have better antepasts of the perfect rest than by that joy and peace which are shed abroad in us by the Holy Ghost ? Communion with God is a chief ingredient in the bliss of the glorified ; and here below, by the Spirit of God, we are enabled to delight ourselves in the Lord, and rejoice in the God of our salvation. Fellowship with the Lord Jesus in all his gracious designs and purposes, and likeness to him in love to God and man, are also chief constituents in our perfected condition before the throne; and these the Spirit of holiness is working in us from day to day. To be pure in heart so as to see God, to be established in character so as to be fixed in righteousness, to be strong in good so as to overcome all evil, and to be cleansed from self so as to find our all in God; are not these, when carried to the full, among the central benedictions of the beatific vision? And are they not already bestowed upon us by that Spirit of glory and of power which even now rests upon us? It is so. In the Holy Spirit we have the things we seek after. In him the flower of heaven has come to us in the bud, the dawn of the day of glory has smiled upon us.

We are not, then, such strangers to the promised blessings as common talk would make us out to be. Many repeat, like parrots, the word, "Eye hath not seen, nor ear heard, neither have entered into the heart of man, the things which God hath prepared for them that love him" (1 Cor. ii. 9); but they fail to add the words which follow in the same Scripture, "but God hath revealed them unto us by his Spirit." What cruelty thus to cut the living child of Scripture in halves! The Holy Spirit has revealed to us what neither eye nor ear has perceived: he has drawn back the curtains, and bidden us see the secrets hidden from ages and from generations. Behold, in the life of God within your soul, the everlasting life which is promised to them that love God. The life of glory is but the continuance and the outgrowth of the life of grace. Behold, in reconciliation through the atoning blood, that celestial peace which is the groundwork of eternal rest. See, in the love of God shed abroad in the believing soul, a foretaste of the fragrance of felicity. Mark, in the immovable security and hallowed serenity of full assurance, a forecast of the infinite repose of Paradise. When our inward joys swell high, and burst into a song, then we hear preludes of the heavenly hallelujahs. If we would know the clusters of Canaan, lo, they are brought to us by those emotions and anticipations, which, under the guidance of the Spirit, have gone, like spies, into the good land, and brought us hence its choicest fruits!

It is not only that we *shall* have an inheritance: but WE HAVE IT. In having the Holy Spirit, we are already put in possession of the land which floweth with milk and honey. "We which have believed do enter into rest" (Heb. iv. 3). "Ye are come unto mount Sion, and unto the city of the living God, and to an innumerable company of angels" (Heb. xii. 22).

What remains for such persons, thus made partakers of a divine inheritance in the Son of God, but that they walk worthy of their high, holy, heavenly calling? "If ye then be risen with Christ, seek those things which are above, where Christ sitteth on the right hand of God" (Col. iii. 1).

Jesus and the Promises

" For all the promises of God in him are yea, and in him Amen, unto the glory of God by us."—2 Cor. i. 20.

JESUS, our Lord, stands for ever connected with the way of the promise. Indeed, he is " the way, the truth, and the life." No man comes to the Faithful Promiser but by Jesus Christ. We could not close this little book without a short chapter upon HIM. Our hope is that the reader will not attempt to obtain any comfort from a word that we have written, or even from the Word of God itself, except as he receives it through Jesus Christ. Apart from him the Scripture itself contains nothing which the soul of man may live upon. This, indeed, is the great fault of many—they search the Scriptures, for in them they think they have eternal life, but they will not come unto Christ, that they might have life. Let us not be of this foolish company ; but let us come to Jesus day by day, knowing that it pleased the Father that in him should all fulness dwell. Only as we know him do we know the light, life, and liberty of the heirs of promise ; and, as surely as we wander from him we roam into bondage. Oh, for grace to abide in him, that we may possess all the good things of the covenant made with us in him !

Jesus is the Gate of the promises. Through him
the Lord is able to enter into gracious engagements
with guilty men.   Until "the seed of the woman"
had been appointed to be the Mediator between
God and man, no messages of comfort could be
sent to the offending race.   God had no word for
sinners till the Word of God undertook to be made
flesh, and to dwell among us.   God could not
communicate his mind of love to men except
through Jesus, the Word.   As God could not come
to us apart from the Messenger of the covenant, so
we could not approach to him except through the
Mediator.   Our fears drive us away from the Holy
One till we see in the Son of God a Brother full of
tender sympathy.   The glory of the divine Trinity
overawes us until we behold the milder radiance of
the Incarnate God.   We come to God through the
humanity of his Son, and especially through that
humanity suffering and dying on our behalf.

Jesus is the Sum of all the promises. When God
promised his Son to be ours, he gave us in him all
things necessary for our salvation.   Every good gift
and every perfect gift will be found within the person, offices, and work of our Redeemer.   All the
promises are "in him."   If you would add them up,
or make a long catalogue of all the blessings which
they secure to us, you may save yourself the pains,
and be happy to know that this is the full total—
the Lord has given us his Son Jesus.   As all
the stars are in the sky, and all the waves are in
the sea, so are all covenant blessings in Christ.   We
cannot think of a real blessing outside of our Lord:

He is all in all. On this thread all pearls are strung: in this casket all gems are contained.

Jesus is the Guarantee of the promises. He that spared not his own Son will deny nothing to his people. If he had ever thought of drawing back, he would have done so before he had made the infinite sacrifice of his Only-begotten Son. Never can there be a suspicion that the Lord will revoke any one of the promises since he has already fulfilled the greatest and most costly of them all. " How shall he not with him also freely give us all things ? "

Jesus is the Confirmer of the promises. They are " in him yea, and in him Amen." His coming into our nature, his standing as our federal Head, and his fulfilling of all the stipulations of the covenant, have made all the articles of the divine compact firm and enduring. Now is it not only kind but just with God to keep his promises to men. Since Jesus has rendered, on man's behalf, a full recompense to the divine honour which sin has assailed, the justice of God unites with his love in securing the carrying out of every word of promise. As the rainbow is our assurance that the world shall never be destroyed by a flood, so is Jesus our assurance that the floods of human sin shall never drown the faithful kindness of the Lord. He has magnified the law, and made it honourable ; he must be rewarded for his soul-travail, and therefore all good things must come to those for whom he died. It would be an unhinging and dislocation of all things if the promises were now to become of none effect after our Lord has done all that was required to make them sure. If we are indeed one with the Lord Jesus Christ, the promises are as sure to us as the love of his Father is to him.

Jesus is the Remembrancer of the promises. He pleads with God on our behalf, and his plea is the divine promise. "He made intercession for the transgressors." For the good things which he has promised the Lord will be enquired of by us that he may do them for us; and that this enquiry may be carried out under the most encouraging circumstances, behold, the Lord Jesus himself becomes the Intercessor for us: for Zion's sake he doth not hold his peace, but day and night he makes remembrance of the everlasting covenant, and of the blood whereby it was sealed and ratified. At the back of every promise stands the living, pleading, and prevailing High-priest of our profession. *We* may forget the faithful promise, but he will not: he will present the incense of his merit, and the engagements of God on our behalf, in that place within the veil where he exercises omnipotent intercession.

Jesus is the Fulfiller of the promises. His first Advent brought us the major part of the blessings which the Lord has foreordained for his own, and his second Advent is to bring us the rest. Our spiritual riches are linked with his ever-adorable person. Because he lives, we live; because he reigns, we reign; because he is accepted, we are accepted. Soon, at his manifestation, we shall be manifested; in his triumph, we shall triumph; in his glory, we shall be glorified. He is himself the Alpha and the Omega of the promises of God : in him we have found life as sinners, in him we shall find glory as saints. If he be not risen, our faith is vain ; and if he come not a second time, our hope is a delusion ; but, since he has risen from the dead, we are justified ; since he will come in the glory of the Father, we also shall be glorified.

READER, WHAT HAST THOU TO DO WITH CHRIST ?

All will depend upon thine answer to this question. Dost thou rest alone in HIM ? Then the Lord has promised to bless thee, and do thee good; and he will surprise thee with the amazing manner in which he will do this unto thee. *Nothing is too good for the Father to give to the man who delights in his Son Jesus.*

On the other hand, art thou trusting to thine own doings, feelings, prayings, and ceremonials ? Then thou art of the works of the law, and thou art under the curse. See what we said of the seed of Hagar, the bondwoman ; and guess what thy portion will be. Oh, that thou wouldst quit the house of bondage, and flee to the home of free grace, and become one whom God will bless

ACCORDING TO THE PROMISE !

God grant this great favour unto thee for the Lord Jesus Christ's sake ! Amen.